RED TAIL PILOTS
IN THE SUNSET

Works by Irv Broughton

Red Tail Pilots in the Sunset
Lovely Company
Through the Flowery Fence
Unto These Skies We Came
The Fires of Tangerine: Poems
Fielding the Cape Cod Past: Poems
Where the Wings Grow:
Conversations with Pioneering Women Pilots
The Levees that Break in the Heart: Novel
The Gracious Afterward: Delta Stories
Gotcha! Watcha! Drugs Are a Trap
The Fart Detective Strikes Again
The Lost Peninsula: Adventures in Florida
The Long Net: Poems about the Great Game of Basketball
ESPN: The Untold Story (with Stuart Evey)
Forever Remembered: The Fliers of World War II
Hangar Talk: Conversations with American Fliers
A Good Man: Fathers and Sons in Poetry and Prose
The Writer's Mind: Interviews with American Authors
Volumes 1–3
Producers on Producing: The Making of Film and Television
The Art of the Interview in Television, Radio and Film
The Blessing of the Fleet: Poems
Surveying: Poems

Plays

Smitten: The Internet Musical
Three to the Heart: A Life with Frank Stanford

RED TAIL PILOTS
IN THE SUNSET

Tuskegee Heroes
Tell Their Stories

Irv Broughton

Open Look Books
Spokane

For more information or to schedule speaking engagements, contact the author at www.awritersweb.com

Interviews with William H. Holloman III and Howard Baugh appeared in *Forever Remembered: The Fliers of WWII*. Copyright © 2001 by Irv Broughton.

Interview with Freddie Hutchins appeared in *Hangar Talk*. Copyright 1998 © by Irv Broughton.

Available from Kindle, Amazon, and other fine booksellers.

ISBN: 978-0-912350-78-3 (paperback)

Cover design by Lilly Ross
Book design by Julie Klein (JKlein-Editor.com)

Printed in the United States of America

Published by Open Look Books, Spokane, Washington

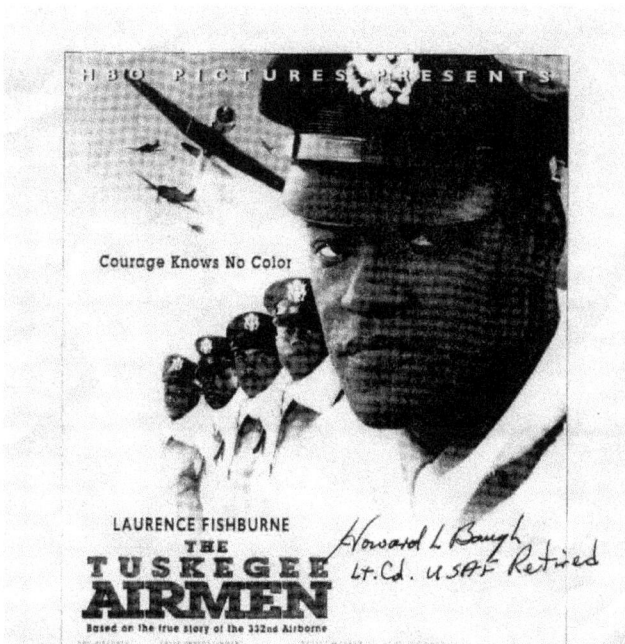

"Red Tail" P-51s of the 332nd Fighter Group

For James Stephens III

Walk that flak, and I pray you'll get there.

—WWII saying

I flew 18 missions in B-17s during the period from March 1945 until the war ended in Europe. During my missions, my aircraft received numerous hits from flak, however, we were lucky, as enemy aircraft never attacked us. I attribute this to the skill of the Tuskegee Airmen, who provided us fighter protection. I was on the March 28, 1945, mission to Berlin, and it was comforting to see their Red Tail P-51s watching over us. I was most fortunate that none of my crew were injured on our missions. The luck of the draw! Those of us who were lucky enough to be escorted by William Holloman III and the Tuskegee Airmen owe them a debt of gratitude.

—Colonel William R. Morton, USAF
Letter to Irv Broughton

Contents

Veteran pilots of the 99th Fighter Squadron stand next to a P-40 Warhawk at an airbase in Italy. L to R: Lieutenant George R. Bolling, Captain Erwin B. Lawrence, and Captain Leon C. Roberts. Courtesy of the National Archives.

Foreword

The Tuskegee Airmen interviews in *Red Tail Pilots in the Sunset* brought back many memories of my father. The interviews echo stories that my father, Maj. Joseph P. Gomer related about his time as a Tuskegee Airman and his subsequent years in the Air Force. He spent much of his later years telling the Tuskegee story in schools, on the radio, in print and in-person interviews. My dad shared stories of his pride in serving his country, yet still facing discrimination in the military and at home, as did these men.

My father was assigned as a Second Lieutenant to the segregated 332 Fighter Group and sent to Ramitelli, Italy, to join the 301st Fighter Squadron. There are many similarities in his stories and of the men in this book. He no doubt knew some of the airmen that were interviewed here.

I am forever proud of the Tuskegee Airmen and their role in the military and their service to their country. I found this book to be an excellent read and rendering.

—A proud daughter of Major Joseph P. Gomer
[name withheld by request]

Tuskegee fliers in training

Introduction

As a child, I devoured the flying publications and sought what I could of them in our small community. I also built model airplanes.

When I interviewed Lee Archer II or William Holloman III, I wasn't surprised to hear that they, like so many kids like me, dreamed of flight and visited those dreams in any way possible. What I could not imagine, or know, was what these African-American fliers faced. The mind shudders to learn that a group of people couldn't walk into a restaurant and belong there, that they faced one humiliation after another. It would take a sit-in and a view of faces down the long length of a counter to assist in the move to change. Before that, there were some brave fliers that would show their brilliance and courage.

I had first learned about the Tuskegee fliers in a minute mention, I believe, actually an obituary, in a southern community newspaper. From that point on, I searched and wanted to know more. I looked for information but found little in my limited spectrum. I may have known they were the first all-Black Fighter Group that set records for efficiency, lowest loss records, in escorting bombers during WWII.

In the interviews with these four remarkable men, I was struck immediately by the generosity and openness, the kindness, and the ready way they would exhilarate their words as they mentioned those they admired, those that influenced them to bravely continue against all odds.

This collection of interviews, *Red Tail Pilots in the Sunset*, means a lot to me. For close to fifty years, I have interviewed, in-depth, a number of fliers, from pioneers to military, all ground breakers who have made aviation history in America, but these four interviews with Tuskegee pilots are clearly among my most cherished of interviews.

My dear grandmother, Evelyn Louise Lyon Broughton, was an aspiring writer who inspired me. At one point, she reached out to Eleanor Roosevelt with a question about writing and, wonderfully, received a letter back.

Eleanor Roosevelt, wife of President Franklin D. Roosevelt. She influenced her husband to support the training of the one thousand Black aspiring pilots at Tuskegee Institute in Alabama. So much for influences and synchronicities in the vastness of the world.

Traits keep rising to the fore in my memories. I will also always remember their warmth and humor, and when I listen to them in the recordings, I love the lilt and grace in their voices, and I am further moved. What these African Americans faced on an almost daily basis stuns the mind and conscience. It is a legacy that lives on in the annals of the vastly accomplished. It was a privilege to have learned from them a little of what they experienced, and to sense their resilience and strength in the face of not just bullets and the scatter of flak. It is understanding that transcends.

In the interviews, I was particularly moved by the story of Freddie Hutchins who, when shot down and brought to a mountain village in Italy, was deemed "a Black Messiah." The Nazis had raided the place of food, and when a fish appeared, the villagers knew who had to have brought the luck upon the village. Only powerful forces could send a giant fish to wash up on shore at such a critical time, a miracle to a starving population.

The Tuskegee fliers went skyward and the sky became their pedestal, a way to communicate so many things about a race, a people. I hope the reader finds in this book something of what I experienced in the very brief interlude of an personal interview.

—Irv Broughton

Howard Baugh, Tuskegee pilot

Chapter 1

Loose Lips Sink Ships and Other Stories: An Interview with Howard Baugh

Howard Baugh entered the U.S. Army Air Corps in March 1942 at Tuskegee Army Air Field, Alabama. He received his pilot wings and commission as a second lieutenant in November of that year. Baugh flew combat missions in the European theater from July 1943 through September 1944. Following WWII, he remained in the air force, finally retiring 1967 after 25 years of active duty.

Baugh was born in Petersburg, Virginia, and attended public schools there and in Brooklyn, New York. He graduated from Virginia State College (now University).

For the interview, we sat down in the kitchen of my house, around an oak table, and Baugh, a man of modesty, strength, and grace, settled into a hard, oak chair, looking as comfortable as if he were in a cockpit.

Tell me, how did you decide to become a Tuskegee pilot?

The idea wasn't to become a Tuskegee pilot. The idea was to learn to fly. I had always been interested in flying. As a teenager, I read many stories about the air war over France and Germany during WWI. I heard an airplane, and I would run out and look up and see what was there. Flying was something that I'd always wanted to do. At that time, of course, the Army Air Corps wasn't taking applications for pilot training from African Americans. As soon as I found out in 1941 that the military had changed its policy, I made application and was fortunate enough to qualify on the written exam and the physical, and to be accepted for pilot training. Then I went to Tuskegee.

What is your earliest memory of Tuskegee?

The earliest memory was the railroad station nearest the base where passengers were let off the train. The station consisted of a small wooden shack about the size of this room. There was—nothing, no stationmaster or anything. The train just let you off and went on. There was no transportation from there, and it was three or four miles from the base. Fortunately, there was a telephone, so you could call the base and get somebody to come out and pick you up.

It wasn't exactly what I expected. It was a total disappointment at first. When I did finally get to the base, I found out that the base was still under construction. The roads had not been paved. There was red clay in the streets, and everywhere you went you picked up the red clay on your feet. Things were crude.

But you got adjusted to it?

Oh, yeah, I got adjusted all right. The biggest adjustment was to the hectic training and the rigorous schedule—classroom, instruction, close-order drill, physical training, etc. The construction people continued to build the base. They paved the streets and completed a lot of 70 buildings while I was in pilot training. Then, by the time I came back from overseas and went to Tuskegee Army Airfield again, I found it had been completely finished.

Although it wasn't mentioned in the movies, a lot of the tough part of the training was the hazing that we got from upperclassmen. And, of course, the training itself was tough. We attended classes for half the day, and we flew the other half. I thought I could learn to fly, and evidently I could, because I didn't have a very difficult time with the airplanes. There were things to remember and things to master, but it went well, and I got along very well with my instructors. I think they were pleased in general with my performance and my progress.

Was there any time you had doubts, though? Did you ever have any doubts?

I think everybody going through there had doubts. We didn't know if we would master the training as quickly as was necessary. We knew that some things could come up and we could make mistakes in the air that would get us eliminated. We saw our classmates being eliminated and knew we could be next. There were doubts right on up to the end.

Did you have any buddies that washed out that you felt really badly about?

Sicily, 1943: Baugh stands next to his
P-40 "Warhawk."

Oh yeah. A fellow from Brooklyn, New York, whom I had known as a teenager, when I was going to high school up there, washed out. He had finished all the training and had gotten so close to graduation that his name was on graduation special order, but for reasons that were never made clear to me, he didn't graduate and didn't receive his commission and his wings.

Was that a racial thing, do you think?

I have no idea. I don't really have any reason to believe it was racial. We were all Black. There were originally 20 cadets in the class. Only four of us graduated. Of course, the instructors at that time were White, because we didn't have any qualified Black instructors at that level of training. We had Black instructors in primary and light airplanes, but after that, we had all White instructors.

What is the biggest misunderstanding that people have about the Tuskegee fliers, in this day and time?

I don't know that they have a misunderstanding. It's just that a lot of people didn't know about us until the movie *The Tuskegee Airmen* came out—not even Black people. The movie was successful in making the public aware of the Tuskegee Airmen. It was a commercial venture that made money. It was entertaining. It was done well. There were a few things that were put in it for dramatic effect, and some license was taken.

Do you wish they didn't put in the fellow crashing in the film?

You have to understand that was for dramatic effect, for the audience. It gives people false ideas, but I don't have any objection to that. The only thing that was objected to by others that I know of was that Black civilian contract pilots were not depicted in the movie. Those that are still alive resent that, since they were an important part of our training.

Tell me about the civilian contract pilots who taught you. Did you have any friends who you knew real well?

We weren't friends with the instructors. I don't think we were supposed to be. We went to the airfield. We lived on campus at that time, at Tuskegee Institute. We were driven to the airfield, and we met our instructors, and we were briefed on what we were going to do individually with the instructor. We got in the airplane and we flew. Then we left the instructors there, and we had no other contact with them.

I was one of the first four replacement pilots for the 99th Fighter Squadron, which had gone overseas a couple of months earlier, in April 1943. I had been a pilot and a second lieutenant for about six months. Three other second lieutenants, also brand-new pilots, and I went down to Camp Patrick Henry, near Newport News, Virginia. They must have been expecting us because they had a great big empty two-story barrack to put us in. We were the only four in the barrack. At the end of the building there was the usual latrine, with all the stools and basins and things right side by side. Of course, we had plenty of room. But the other White junior officers were housed in a similar building, all jammed up in double-deck beds on both floors, with the same-sized latrine. They had to line up to go to the bathroom, and when they did, they probably had to sit on a warm seat.

Everybody was confined to the base because the brass didn't trust us to keep our mouths shut if we went off base. The saying in those days was "Loose Lips Sink Ships!"

The military wasn't going to give us an opportunity to say where we were going, when we were going, and what ship we were going on. Ironically, we didn't know anything in the first place. But everybody was confined to the base. One of our pilots didn't like that idea and wanted to get off base. So he went to see the base commander and told him he'd like to have passes for the four of us to go off base in the evening, until we shipped out. He got the usual lecture about loose lips sinking ships and that everybody was confined. He said, "But sir, we need to socialize with somebody, and there aren't any Black women on this base to socialize with." The guy said, "Well, I'm sorry." He said, "Well, if we can't socialize with Black women, we'll have to socialize with the White women." That night, and every night thereafter until we shipped out, the four of us were the only ones that had passes to go off the base! He forgot all about the sinking of the ships and the loose lips. He had to protect the White women, who were quite capable of protecting themselves, I'm sure. That's a true story.

When we got on shipboard, we still had to be segregated. They put all the junior officers down in the hold of the ship, sleeping on hammocks, stacked one on top of the other. They had to line up to use the washbasins. In order to segregate us, they put is in the two state rooms on one of the upper decks of the ship— with built-in bunks and wash facilities right in the cabin. As it turned out, we had some of the best accommodations on the ship because we were Black [*laughs*]. When I told that story on C-SPAN, I started out by saying, "Most often, segregation is cruel. But sometimes it's ridiculous, and that was ridiculous."

Was there any time you got out of the plane and took that mask off and shocked people with the fact that you were Black?

That mostly happened back in the States. In the late 1940s and early 1950s, we would fly around the country to different air force bases, and people were surprised to see a Black pilot climb out of an airplane— especially if he had a White crew. In the 1950s, I was assigned to an outfit at Sacramento, California, McClellan Air Force Base, and our job was to ferry airplanes all over the States and overseas. I had occasion to lead a group of about eight B-26s down to Lima, Peru. After we picked the airplanes up in Mobile, Alabama, we flew down to Miami and spent the night there. Then we flew to Panama and spent a couple of days there, waiting for the weather down in Lima to clear up enough for us to be able to land. All the airplanes had two crew members on them—an engineer and a pilot—so we had a total of 16 people, and I was the only Black in the group, but I was their leader and I was a major; everybody else was of lower rank.

We were asked to land at three o'clock in the afternoon, because that was the time that the president of Peru was going to be there to see the airplanes come in. We landed on time. The next morning, the newspaper made a great deal out of the fact that this Black guy was leading these White people, with no sign of rank visible [laughs].

Who was their commander?

I had one of those little envelope hats on, so when I went to greet the president, I took it off and put in it my side pocket. The photographers were there and they didn't see any rank at all. (That was before we started putting the rank on our flying suits.) As a consequence, I didn't have any name or rank showing. I was just another guy in a flying suit. They were surprised that a Black guy could do this. And I'm sure that occurred because of the stories they had heard prior to our arrival, over the years, of how Blacks were treated in this country.

What was your proudest moment flying?

I was leading a dive-bombing mission down in the valley between mountains. When we got over the target area, we found that clouds obscured the target. The peaks of the mountains were sticking up through the clouds. I wasn't accustomed to going to a target with a bomb and not dropping it on the target. We could have gone out to sea and thrown it "bombs away," but we didn't want to do that. So I was looking at my map really carefully, checking the peaks. I was able to determine that if I could find a hole, I could find the target. I went under the clouds and left the other airplanes on top of the clouds, circling. I weaved my way through the valleys, under the clouds, around the mountains, found the target, put my bomb on it, and then zoomed up through the clouds. Then the other pilots in the flight were able to dive down through the hole I had made with my bomb. That was fantastic!

Our dive-bombing targets included artillery gun emplacements like that. Once I was scraping along the road, instead of across the road, as we were taught, and we went back for a second pass, which we shouldn't have done. We were told not to do that, but we did. The fellow that was flying with me got hit. He had enough airspeed to zoom up to an altitude to where he could bail out, but he was captured and went to a POW camp in Germany and spent the rest of the war there. His name was Lewis Smith. He died a couple of years ago. Lewis and I both had motorcycles over there. He had gone to a dump where they dumped old vehicles and had picked up just enough damaged parts from Harley-Davidson motorcycles to put one together. It was an unregistered vehicle that he owned. The government didn't know he owned it. (They probably would have taken it away from him.) But he owned it, and when he was shot down, I inherited his motorcycle. The motorcycle I had was an Italian motorcycle, a Bianca, and his was better, so I took over his. I don't know what happened to the Bianca.

So, what did you do with this? Did you terrorize the hills?

No, we'd just drive around to the different villages and visit with the people and see the countryside, in Sicily and in Italy. When we moved from Sicily to Italy, we just put the Harley-Davidson and the Bianca on the C-47 and brought them with us.

What's the most fun you had with the local people over there?

We didn't have much fun with the local people. In Naples, we did have what they called a rest camp of our own. It was up over a hill overlooking Naples Bay and the Isle of Capri. We could visit there in the evening and get drinks, and some of the fellows would have dates with girls. I was married at the time, but it was such a nice diversion for some of the guys. Some flew combat in dress uniforms so that when they came back from a mission, they could go straight to town without going back to the barracks and changing clothes. It was so much better than fighting the war on the ground. We could go up and fly for an hour and a half or two hours and then come back. We were free until the next day. We had a good time, except for times we were being shot at.

Talk about the remarkable record in terms of the escorts.

The four of us joined the 99th Pursuit Squadron at Licata, Sicily. We were in the 12th Air Force, which was a tactical air force. Our job was to support the ground troops. We did dive-bombing and strafing in proximity, but in front of friendly forces. We had to be precise in our navigation so that we didn't dive-bomb or strafe our own forces. I felt confident that we were able to navigate well enough to find the right targets.

When the 332nd Fighter Group, with three squadrons, came overseas, they were stationed at Capodichino Air Base near Naples, Italy, where we were also stationed. They were assigned P-39s. Their mission was shore patrol, on the lookout for enemy aircraft and submarines. I don't know if they found any.

Although the 99th Pursuit Squadron was flying out of the same airfield as the 332nd Fighter Group, the 99th remained with the 79th Fighter Group, flying P-40s. We continued our tactical mission, dive-bombing, strafing, and flying cover over the Anzio beachhead.

After I'd been over there a year, we were moved over to the east coast of Italy and given an air base. We occupied the whole thing. The four squadrons joined the other three squadrons to make us the only four-squadron fighting group over there. All the other fighting groups had three squadrons. But they didn't know what else to do with us. We were then assigned to the 15th Air Force, which was a strategic air force. They had fighter groups and bomber groups. We had P-51 Mustangs. The heavy bombers were B-17s and B-24s, doing high-altitude bombing of places in Germany, Austria, northern Italy, Vienna, and in Ploieşti, and places like that. Then we went over to the Ploieşti oil fields in Romania a couple of times.

We escorted the bombers over there. Sometimes the missions were so long that we had to use two waves of fighters to escort one wave of bombers, because the bombers were so much slower than the fighters. On the way, we had to weave over them to stay with them. Then we'd get out so far, and then we had to leave the bombers to come back in a straight line, instead of weaving, to get back to base before we ran out of fuel. Before we could leave the bombers, another fighter group would come up and take over the escort work.

The flights to Ploeşti were memorable to me. Not just because it was a long flight, but we would fly at high altitudes, sometimes up to 35,000 feet. Our airplanes weren't adequately heated. We had cabin heat off the manifold, but it was cold by the time it got to the cockpit. We actually had some frostbitten feet; luckily, that never happened to me.

Over Ploeşti, the escort fighters—that's us—did not have to stay with the bombers, because enemy fighters could not attack the bombers on the bomb run because of danger from anti-aircraft fire—their own anti-aircraft fire—from the ground. The bombers had to start their bomb run on what they called the Initial Point [IP], when the bombardier takes over the control of the airplane to be sure that it's straight and level and he can align his bombsight to get the bombs on the target. When that's going on, the bombers are sitting ducks for the anti-aircraft fire. There was so much anti-aircraft fire over Ploești on each bomb run that it looked like a big, big black cloud that they had to fly through. Although it's said that we lost no bombers to enemy fighters, I did see a lot of bombers get shot down by anti-aircraft fire over Ploieşti. I saw people at 25,000 feet, or above, bail out of airplanes. Some of them had their parachutes on fire, and they'd plummet to the ground. And of course they wouldn't die until they hit. That allowed someone a long time to think about their home and to think about their life—a horrible way to go.

Of course, there were 10 to 12 crew members on each airplane. Every time they lost a bomber, that many people went down. What the bombers were doing with the four-engine airplanes was a lot more dangerous than what we were with the single-engine airplanes.

There were times when I did foolish things with the airplanes, not just on the fighters, but even with the B-25s, which was a two-engine bomber. We were stationed at a base in Italy, and at the time they were putting down tar on the runway. We had a mission to do. I made my takeoff, and when I did, I flew right over the workers. They fell face-down in the tar. By the time I got to the base, there was a new regulation that we couldn't do that anymore.

What did you like about the P-40?

There was very little to like about it. First of all, when you first got in it, it was frightening. It was a big leap from our advanced trainer and finishing pilot training to getting in the P-40. You see, the trainer had two seats. You had an instructor on the first time you took off. Modern-day fighters have fighters with two seats, although the combat airplane—the tactical airplane—is a one-seat airplane. There are two-seat trainers for training in an airplane you first fly. Also, there are flight simulators to train you to fly the airplane before you get in it the first time. That wasn't true with the P-40 and P-51. The first time you got in the P-40 or P-51 or P-39 or P47, you soloed it. After studying the operational manual, you got in the airplane, sat in there for a while to familiarize myself with the cockpit, and started the engine. Off you went.

Do you remember your solo in the P-40?

Oh, yeah. It was hair-raising. It was the first time that I had an airplane that had a friction lock on the throttle. A friction lock is a wheel on the throttle that you can tighten or loosen, so that the throttle would either be hard to move or easy to move. I forgot about the friction lock and, as it turned out, mine happened to be loose. So when I went down the runway with my hand off the throttle to lift the gear—the throttle flew back! I had to take my hand back up again without getting the gear up and push the throttle forward again. The right hand is on the control column, and I could not turn that loose. So here I am in a dilemma. Every time I took my hand off the throttle to get the wheels up, the throttle would come back and the engine would slow down, and I'd start sinking. I had to push the throttle up again. I had to wait before I got a pretty good altitude, with the wheels down, before I could turn the throttle loose and let the throttle slide back—retract the wheels and then push the throttle up again and tighten the friction lock with my other hand.

Tell me about your solo in the P-51.

The solo in the P-51 wasn't any problem because the cockpit and the handling of it were actually a little bit easier than a P-40. We were accustomed to flying the high-powered airplanes with the power that the P-51 had. That was no big transition. There were slight differences between the two airplanes. The main difference in the P-51 was that it had much more power and that it had a four-bladed prop instead of a three-bladed prop. It had a lot more power, so you also had to have more torque. On the takeoff roll with high rpm, the torque would try to pull the airplane to the left. The P-51 had a steerable tail wheel. The rudder pedals were used to steer the tail wheel to keep the plane on the centerline until the airspeed was built up. The idea was to get up to enough speed so that you had air going over your vertical stabilizer and so that you could maintain direction by using the rudder rather than the tail wheel. You had to get a pretty good speed with [the] tail wheel still on the ground. If you didn't do that, the propeller would pull the plane right off the runway.

We had been trained in the other airplanes, in stalls, to become familiar with the airplane and build up confidence in it. You'd get up into a power-off stall, a power-on stall, a flaps-down stall, a wheels-down stall, and stuff like that. I was in a P-40 and wanted to go through this series of stalls and build up my confidence in the airplane to get familiar with it. I did all my stalls okay and recovered from them. When you stall an airplane, that means you get down just below the flying speed. You don't have enough forward motion to keep the airplane flying, so the airplane falls, and you recover. So I decided I wanted to do a power-on stall. With the normal cruise power, I pulled the nose up, and the airplane climbed and climbed and climbed. I got up to around

15,000 feet before the airplane stalled. Then the torque took over on the right when the airplane lost flying speed, and it put me into a violent power-on spin. It threw me all around the cockpit. I finally got to the place where I could pull the throttle off and straighten out the airplane. I must have lost six or seven thousand feet. It was a good thing I was that high to start with. Of course, I never tried that again! That occurred at Tuskegee, when I was still transitional in the airplane. I never told anybody about it, either.

It seems like you had a few secrets back then.

Oh, I did. I did some things that I didn't want people to know about.

You weren't the only one, though?

No, I certainly wasn't.

Why do you think it was that you were secretive?

I was afraid really that I would get eliminated. That it would get out that I had done something stupid. Something stupid like that would get you eliminated. No one wanted to be eliminated. I think it would have crushed me, personally.

Do you remember any unusual situations while you were teaching?

I was never comfortable while teaching academic subjects in the classroom. I was always confident and comfortable teaching flying to cadets, teaching instruments, giving instrument check rides, and things like that. But in the classroom, I felt that my being there as an instructor was a gross injustice to the students.

That isn't entirely logical, is it?

No, it's not. The last couple of years I've gone back up to Howard University on invitation where I was an assistant professor of air science. Howard was my first ROTC assignment, starting back in 1946. I stayed there for three years. Many of the people who were students in the ROTC program at that time went on active duty, and three of them became generals. They think that I was the greatest thing that ever happened to them, as a role model. I didn't think that; I told all of them that they give me credit I wasn't due. I still think that.

You're sure you're not just a little bit modest?

No, that's not it at all. I really, honestly feel that way. When I got the second assignment down to Tennessee State, I was a good commander. I had some excellent ROTC instructors working for me. They did the bulk of the instruction. I didn't do much, because I wasn't comfortable with it. I didn't have to do too much, so I did the minimum I could get away with. We had three or four pilots assigned there. I was the only one that would take the cadets out and go fly with them. I'd take them up in a T-33. That was a two-seat single-engine jet trainer. I'd take them up and fly them one at a time. I'd also get a C-47, which is a civilian DC-3, and we'd load 15 or 20 of them and take them places. I was always the pilot. They admired me for that. They felt I was a role model in presenting examples for them, and a lot of them went on active duty and did well—a lot better than I did.

A four-star general that was in the program is still on active duty. He stood up in front of a big audience of about one thousand people at our convention a couple of years ago and pointed me out. He had me stand up and gave my name and said that I taught him all he knows. I replied that, because he said that, he had the greatest sense of humor in the world [*laughs*].

You seem to be a people person.

I don't let things upset me. A little girl did something that she thought would make me mad. I said that, when you get to know me better, you will find that I never get mad at anybody about anything. That's the truth. I don't have any reason to get mad with people. They may do things I don't like, but getting mad only hurts me.

People ask me, after I give them my story about the segregation and the treatment we got and the prejudice that we encountered, whether I'm bitter about any of that. Bitterness only hurts the person who is bitter. It doesn't hurt anybody else. It's foolish to be bitter. There's nobody around now for me to be bitter at. That was the way back then. If you understand the social conditions in the

United States at that time, understanding that will ease your mind about bitterness. You understand what the situation was, so you don't let it bother you.

Did you fly after retirement?

I didn't fly as a pilot after retirement. First of all, I was raising a family, had a wife and three kids. Civilian flying is expensive, and I never felt I had the money for it. Then a couple of years ago, after my wife passed, I thought I might like to get back into flying again, so I went out and took a couple of lessons in a Cessna 170. I found that the whole time I was up flying the airplane that I was thinking that I'd rather be on the golf course. I didn't understand that for a long time. After giving a lot of thought, I determined that the reason that I didn't care for it was because that kind of flying didn't have a purpose. When I was in the air force, every time I used an airplane it had a purpose: to go someplace or do something or carry somebody.

You've had quite a remarkable life.

I think that I've had a wonderful life. I've

had wonderful experiences. I say to a lot of people that life treats me better than I deserve. That's close to the truth. Life is good to me. I've been really fortunate.

William H. Holloman III, Tuskegee pilot

Chapter 2

Of the Many Ways He Served:
An Interview with
William Holloman III

On his 18th birthday, William H. Holloman III applied to the Army Air Corps for the pilot training program. The date was August 21, 1942. He would graduate as second lieutenant pilot from Tuskegee Army Airfield, Alabama.

In the interview, Holloman talks about the indignities of racial intolerance. Though he expresses that race had not been an issue to any great extent when he was growing up in a sheltered environment in St. Louis, he would find things different almost from the moment he stepped onto a train headed for training at Keesler Field in Biloxi, Mississippi.

Holloman has served as a pilot in three wars: World War II, Korea, and Vietnam. He flew P-40s, P-47s, and P-51s during WWII, and after the war was over, he stayed in the military until 1947. From there, he attended St. Louis University in engineering for a year before returning to the Army Air Corps as a fighter pilot with his old unit, the 332nd Fighter Group, which later became a separate branch of the U.S. Air Force.

The appeal of academe struck again in 1950, and he returned to school at the University of California at Berkeley to study architecture. It was while he was there that he had a reserve assignment with SAC (Special Agent in Command) that led to his recall because of the Korean Conflict. He had sustained a knee problem that kept him out of fighters and thus prevented him from getting into a tactical fighter unit. As a consequence, he was assigned to MATS with various duties as a pilot for medical evacuation and air rescue in Korea. It was during this period that he became the first Black helicopter pilot in the air force.

After the Korean War, he sought his fortune as a commercial pilot. Many companies, in answering letters, said he was qualified and wanted to interview him. But when they interviewed him and saw the color of his skin, they had plenty of excuses. He sued and won a judgment in one such situation.

Over the next couple of years, he had jobs in helicopter training and then crop dusting in Central America; that experience led to his receiving an offer to go to work as a pilot for Pacific Western Airlines in Vancouver, British Columbia. It didn't take Holloman long to make his decision; he didn't even ask how much money he would be making.

As an expert in aircraft accident investigations, safety, and standards, he was sought by Army Aviation for service in Vietnam as early as 1963. With 15 years of active military service in the army, the air force, and the army again, he nonetheless said he would go to Vietnam, but only if they would keep him for five years so he would qualify for retirement. An arrangement was worked out by late 1966, and Holloman joined a new unit for deployment to Vietnam. After 13 months in Vietnam, he was assigned to USAREUR (U.S. Army Europe), where he retired in 1972.

His honors include a Congressional Gold Medal. He retired from the U.S. Army as a lieutenant colonel, having flown over 17,000 hours in his illustrious career.

Despite a myriad of setbacks, William H. Holloman III seems sanguine about it all, a tribute to his courage and full confidence.

What was your earliest interest in flight?

I had a neighbor, whose name I believe was Bonnet, who was a kind of big brother to his own younger brother and those of us his age. In the mid-'30s, he taught us how to build model airplanes, related some about the history of aviation, and often told us stories about World War I warplanes, the early barnstormers, and, of course, the feats of famous Charles Lindbergh and his solo transatlantic flight. It was exciting.

How did you view a fight career as a Black man? Was it a difficult thing to do?

I don't think I saw any real obstacles in my desires to fly. It just seemed like it would be fun and exciting to soar like the eagles. I used to go out to Lambert, St. Louis's airport, just to watch airplanes.

Back in those days, if you didn't make bus connections, you had a long wait or had to walk the last two miles to the airport. I was always too impatient to wait, so I walked. I spent considerable time just walking around watching people working on planes and asking questions. I finally talked my way into a job there around 1937.

What was that?

One guy paid me 10 cents an hour to clean up around the hangar, wash airplanes, and do other simple tasks. That was big bucks back then, and I was happy being able to touch those little planes. The job came about from my continually asking him for a ride in a plane. He had told me that it would cost four or five dollars. Of course, I told him I didn't have that kind of money. I figured if I asked my parents for money for something like that, they would think I was crazy and laugh at me. You know, people were still living in the lean years of the 1929 crash. At any rate, I saved money from my newspaper route and what I was making in the hangar working for these guys. The first time I got in an aircraft, I was charged a day's work just to sit there for about 15 minutes. I must have been the joke of the hangar.

Do you remember your first flight there?

Oh, yeah! It was an open-cockpit bi-wing aircraft. I don't remember the type of aircraft, but it was a real thrill. The pilot pointed out landmarks as we flew over the area and did all kinds of maneuvers I would come to learn in later years. The first time I went up, I felt like my heart was going to go right through the top of my head. I hung onto the aircraft for dear life and prayed I would get back on the ground in one piece. Yet once we were on the ground, I was ready to go again.

It changed your life?

It changed my life. But what's interesting is the fact that I must have gone three more years before I got into another airplane. Finally, in 1940, a friend of mine told me how he had been up in an airplane.

He said, "Come over to Illinois and you can go up for four dollars." His older brother, also a flying enthusiast, accompanied us to Park Airfield in Illinois, which was later to become Park Air College during World War II.

What did you ride in?

It was an Aeronca, which was a two-seater. We were in the air for about 30 or 40 minutes. I sat next to the pilot and handled the controls. I didn't think I'd ever learn to fly, because I was having difficulty just keeping the plane straight. I was almost 16 years old and as a result of that ride, I joined the Civil Air Patrol [CAP].

This was the period where I first became cognizant of the racial issue. My CAP unit was the only one to which the Black cadets, referred to then as Negroes, were assigned.

What did you learn while in the CAP?

We studied basic ground school subjects such as aerodynamics, aircraft mechanics, meteorology, and navigation.

Do you remember anything unique about your instructor?

No, except that, when he left during the Battle of Britain, we heard that he had gone to Canada to join the Royal Canadian Air Force.

A number of the older fellows in the unit followed the same procedure. In fact, in 1941, I had written to the Royal Canadian Air Force inquiring about their qualifications. I had heard that a person could join there at 17 and that high school graduates met their educational requirements. However, I think my main reason for inquiring was that Canada was involved in the war in Europe, and there was something exciting about being a fighter pilot. I couldn't even drive, but flying never seemed dangerous to me. So, in a way, he apparently planted the seed about the possibilities of flying in Canada.

What did your parents think about flying?

My father had been the first to take my brothers and me to Lambert Field to see an airshow in the early 1930s, so I know he had some curiosity about flight. He had an interest in looking at planes, but to fly in one, that was out of the question. I often attempted to talk him into going for a ride with me, but he always had a reason for putting it off. Now, my mother was another matter. When I finally told her about my second flight out of Park in Illinois, she went through the roof.

What did she say?

It would be simpler to tell you what she didn't say. She said, "Those things can fall out of the sky and kill you!" When I was leaving for combat in World War II, she said, "Remember to fly low and not too fast." They both had different reactions when I got the papers back from Canada.

What was that?

My mother wasn't about to sign any papers. There was no discussion. I was just a child, and she was not going to let me pull a stupid stunt like going to war to get killed, trying to show off.

Your father wouldn't sign them, either?

I think up until high school, I had been giving my parents trouble in school. My father made the comment that my attention span was too short for me to learn how to fly an airplane. He also led me to believe that he did not think I was smart enough—he somewhat ridiculed me about my desire.

What did he say?

Well, he just said, "You don't have what it

takes to fly"—or something to that effect. He challenged me. He said, "You don't have the intelligence." He also commented that he had never seen a Negro pilot and he didn't know if there were any. I told him that I did know two Black pilots, that my squadron leader in the CAP was a pilot, as was his replacement.

That was a pretty valuable piece of information for you to give him.

Yes. He even met my second squadron leader when he came by my school to attempt to interest some other boys in flying in late December 1941 or early 1942. He had been in the neighborhood, so he used the opportunity to talk to a half-dozen kids there, but only one, Doug Seals, joined the CAP squadron. Anyway, I lived right down the street from school, so as he was walking back to catch the streetcar, I spotted my dad coming home from work and introduced them. They talked for a while and my dad thanked him for working with me and the other kids, and I believe my dad invited him to the American Legion, to Tom Powell Post. But my father really wasn't disinterested. He said years later, after I came back from the war, that he had prodded me into doing something in which I showed some interest by taking the negative approach and telling me that I didn't have the ability. His prodding prompted me to say to myself, "I'll show you."

He used to tell the guys at the Legion that had it not been for him, I wouldn't have had the determination to make it. He was very proud of that fact. When I first graduated from flight school and came home—so the first day—he took me down to the Legion to show me off to his buddies.

Had he served in the military?

Yes, he had seen service with the 93rd Infantry Division in France during World War I. You know, our city produced a large number of Black airmen during the war. I remember James McCullin Jr., whose mother ran the candy store right on the corner from our school, was the first to sign up for pilot training in St. Louis, Missouri. James was one of the first African Americans who lost his life while flying in the war.

Another pilot I knew well was Wendell

Pruitt, who had completed pilot training before I went in. His brother, Luther, who lived a few doors from us, worked with my cousin. Wendell looked sharp in that uniform, and I was determined to be just like him.

What was the hardest transition to the Tuskegee Institute, when you got there?

My ignorance of racial practices in the South. When I left St. Louis, there were four of us that left together for Keesler Field, Biloxi, Mississippi, on the train. It was a Pullman car, and we were in a four-person parlor. We had the freedom of the train from St. Louis to Evansville, Indiana. When the train left Evansville, the conductor came in and told us we had to move to the coach car up front. We explained that our tickets were for this parlor compartment to Mobile, Alabama, and that we had been paid for by the government. John Squires told him we were not going to move. There was much discussion on the matter, and after intervention by some army official, we were permitted to stay put. Sometime after the matter was settled, and before reaching Nashville, Tennessee, we all went to the dining car to eat, as we had done from St. Louis to Evansville, and were refused service. Again, it was pointed out that we had government-paid meal tickets and were entitled to eat. At this point, we were told we would have to wait before colored passengers were served. When we returned again, there was this curtain up which they sat us behind for our meal. It was very degrading. We felt apprehension and fear. I told myself anything was worth going through just to get an opportunity to fly. After our meal, we were told to stay in our parlor. As I recall, when we arrived at Nashville, Tennessee, the conductor attempted to move us to the Jim Crow car again, and even called for the military police [MP] to force us to move, but they left us there until the next morning, at which time they took the Pullman car off the train and informed us that there was no space in the remaining Pullman cars. We were forced to move to the Jim Crow car for Blacks, in coach, but were still permitted to go to the dining car, with its curtain, for our meals. I think one of the more depressing things about the whole incident was that our uniforms were nice, clean and neatly pressed, when we left

St. Louis. After all, we were very proud of the way we looked and that we were embarking on a venture to serve our country. In that Jim Crow car, right behind the engine, believe me, it was hot. With the windows open, the soot from that engine blew into the car. By the time we got off the train in Biloxi, we looked like death warmed over. You couldn't tell what color those uniforms were. You must understand, here we were, four 18-year-olds, and for the first time in our lives we were far away from our parents, friends, and home.

The excitement of being near military aircraft and the joy of future dreams some-what offset the disgust and anger of a racist system that required young Black Americans to endure such treatment. At any rate, the trucks picked us up and took us to Keesler Field, Mississippi, where we spent the next three or four weeks.

Do you remember anything unusual about being at Tuskegee?

In CTD class there were six from St. Louis—only Fischer didn't make it to pre-flight. He remained at the Institute after our class left to begin our first phase of training at Tuskegee.

My closest friend was washed out in Primary, so the remaining four graduated and went on to fly combat in Italy. You must understand, we were so submerged in our own survival and completing the course that we had little time to worry or help people outside our class.

We were all young kids—many had no college education—which required us to go through one semester of college at Tuskegee Institute—now Tuskegee University—to prepare us for the strenuous training ahead. We went to school all day and studied half the night for about two months. We were in a college environment, yet we were controlled. By this I mean we had to march everywhere we went, to and from class and mess. There were only military students of a single class in each course or classroom. No other college students from the university. They didn't give us very much free time. There was at least one girl there whom I knew from St. Louis. She provided an introductory link to other female students on campus.

Any funny stories about trying to see her or any other girl or any outrageous punishment for trying to see girls?

Nothing that I can remember off the top of my head. We were free after Saturday inspection until bed check on Sunday, so we had plenty of time to attend movies, dances, church, and other social interactions. You must understand, we were there to learn, and failure to comply meant being eliminated from the program. I have heard stories of fellows in the girls' dorm and about others slipping out all night, but I have no direct knowledge of such conduct.

Did you have any friends that didn't make it? It was a demanding experience.

Someone was leaving all the time for failure to keep up with the academic pace or the inability to adjust to the discipline demanded of any such military personnel.

You flew in three wars. Is there anything that sticks out in your mind from World War II?

I think most of us were excited about getting into combat. We were a cocky group, all under 21, and thinking we were the best pilots in the world, able to out-fly any enemy pilot. We felt this after having just completed nearly 130 hours in the P-47.1 think probably one of the most disappointing things we had to learn was that our commander wouldn't let us go off chasing German planes.

Our early missions were bomber escorts, and we had to stay with our bombers unless they attacked by German fighters. Even if we sighted German fighters and wanted to go after them, our instructions, in no uncertain terms, were that unless the planes attacked the bombers, we were to leave them alone. If you consider the tactics involved, those planes were probably sitting out there to lure us away and leave the bombers uncovered, so they could have another group of fighters, not seen by us, ready to attack the unprotected bombers. At that time, some pilots may have been somewhat unhappy about not being able to go after those planes, but sticking to mission plans paid off in the long run and saved bombers.

Years later, after some research had been conducted, we found out that our fighter group had the distinction of never losing a bomber to enemy aircraft. That, as the records have revealed, was quite a feat.

What other accomplishments of the Tuskegee Airmen stand out in your mind?

I remember Easter Sunday, 1945. "The Red Tails," flying the North American P-51, shot down 13 German fighters while losing only one. And the pilot of the plane we lost, after bailing out, was home by dinner. I think the unique thing about this was that they confirmed 13 that day, and then went out the next day and shot down 12 more. I thought that was a record, but in doing my research on our unit, I discovered that the 99th Pursuit Fighter Squadron had matched that sometime prior to my arrival in combat. Another mission of note was when we covered the 5th Bomb Wing's B-17s on the raid to Berlin, the longest raid for the 15th Air Force. This mission taxed our P-51 fighters to the limit of range, though we had 110-gallon external fuel tanks.

The job of 332nd Fighter Group was to escort the bombers to a point southwest of Berlin, where they would be picked up by another fighter group that would escort them over the target. That group was late, and the Red Tails were directed to stay with the bombers for their run over the target. On that particular raid, the Red Tails shot down three German jet fighters. That was significant, since the numbers I have indicated that the 15th Air Force's five fighter groups destroyed eight German jet fighters during the war.

The 332nd accounted for three on a single mission. What frightened you the most?

At first, it was the flak. In fact, the Germans threw that stuff up like people throwing rice at a wedding—it was so thick. Our tactic was to change direction and altitude continually so their guns could not get a fix on our planes. Frequently, planes returned to base with holes from those guns—it seemed like part of a day's mission. I think probably the most frightened I had been was when we were on a fighter sweep in central Germany near Nuremberg. We had spotted this convoy on a road below, moving in the right direction.

Our mission was to take out all traffic moving south by highway, rail, and barge.

Anyway, we spotted a convoy of three large trucks with trailers, traveling along with four or five smaller trucks, moving southeast. We spread out, lined up on them, and dropped down to attack. As we were going in at treetop level, the sides of the big trailers dropped away, revealing their big guns. We kept boring in. We didn't have much choice at this point. I often think of that and compare it to the experience of the 332nd when they were attacking the destroyer. We couldn't turn because we would expose the underside of our aircraft to the guns. We continued the pass, firing away. I guess I was maybe 20 or 30 feet above their guns when I flew over them, firing like crazy. One shell put a large hole in my left wing, while another blew away part of one of the blades of my prop. The shell that went through my left wing was a cannon shell of some type and must have been equipped with a delayed fuse, because it didn't explode when it hit the aircraft. It just made a big hole, but it exploded some 50–100 feet above me. Shrapnel fell on me, inflicting my plane with additional holes.

My gosh, that stuff raining down could have knocked you out of the air?

I guess so, but it was over in a second. While reaching for altitude, I started screaming, "I'm hit! I'm hit! I'm hit!" As I climbed, I slid the canopy back, preparing to bail out. By the time I had reached 700 or 800 feet, I was ready to jump. By then, the aircraft was shaking as if it was going to come apart any second. I stood up in the seat to bail out, but I guess I got chicken at that point, because I said to myself, "This is a good aircraft. This thing is still flying—maybe I can put some distance between here and being a prisoner of war."

I sat back down, strapped myself back in, and kept climbing. By the time I got to 5,000 feet, I was headed south and feeling a little better about my situation. I remember one of my buddies escorting me home—there were three other aircraft with me. They said I was flying so fast they were having a hard time keeping up with me. They could see my plane vibrating and kept warning me, "If you don't slow down, that thing is going to come apart!" [*laughs*].

What did you say?

I said, "I'm just trying to get over the Alps." I was trying to get as much altitude as possible. You have to realize that I was in this situation for the better part of two hours. A lot of things go through your mind in that time. The aircraft was very unstable, and I kept looking out there at that gaping hole in my wing. I prayed a lot. I continued to move the controls, as I attempted to check the aircraft's maneuverability. Every time I moved the controls rapidly, it began to shudder and I would lose some control. I soon learned to make maneuvers very gingerly. By the time I got to 17,000 feet and over the Alps, I could see the Adriatic Sea and our British rescue people giving us radar vectors. Then I began to calm down and assess my situation and plan for what might be a crash landing at home base.

When I arrived home, I was able to get the gear down and locked, and with the crash crew standing by, I landed without incident.

I think one of the amazing things is that our mechanics and crew chiefs were so proficient, thorough, and creative, which always gave me great confidence when I climbed into my plane. After I had landed, they pulled that P-51 into a revetment, assessed the damage, and said it could be repaired. They replaced the left wing, put on a new prop, patched all the holes, and had it ready to fly the next morning. You know, we had superb crew chiefs and maintenance personnel. The work they did getting my aircraft back in the air was just one example of the abilities and teamwork demonstrated by Black airmen. General Hap Arnold, commanding general of Army Air Forces, had reported to the War Department that Blacks would never be able to do the maintenance work to keep the proposed Black pilots in the air.

Their accomplishments and the success of our unit have certainly proven him wrong. By the way, the rest of the flight destroyed those guns and knocked out the trucks.

What other memory stands out about the war?

We had been on stand-down for a couple of days, preparing to move to a new location farther north, near Cattolica. We knew something was developing, but we didn't know what. Of course, mind you, I was not flying anyway. I had been injured in a motorcycle accident and was temporarily off flight status. Since I could not fly and I felt somewhat adventuresome, another pilot and I, really out of curiosity, acquired a jeep to drive up to the new location. After scouting that site and hearing that the German forces were pushed some 200 or 300 miles farther north and were retreating rapidly, we decided to continue on northwest. We somehow managed to pass through our lines, and after scrounging some gas, we ended up near Bologna about 2 p.m. As we were driving down the street, we noticed there were no Americans or American vehicles; we saw German vehicles instead. We concluded they were vehicles taken over by American forces. After deciding to see if we could get something to eat, we parked the jeep in front of what appeared to be a hotel, got out to walk into the place, and these German officers came walking out. They saluted us and we saluted them back. You can imagine our surprise. Why, here we are still at war with them. They got into their command car and they drove off.

Within the next 48 hours, peace would be declared, and maybe they already knew something we didn't, I don't know, but I can tell you, seeing a German officer face-to-face kind of left my heart in my mouth, and I began to shake. We got back into our jeep and made tracks back to where we belonged. Something else we discussed was, what if they had drawn their weapons and attempted to fire at us?

You weren't unarmed?

No, we always carried .45s. The point is that we had gone beyond the point where we had permission to go, and where we found ourselves in an embarrassing situation without orders or anything. So, as I said, we climbed back into our jeep and got the heck out of there. While going back to Ramitelli Airfield, Italy, we were stopped twice and questioned each time. We managed to convince the military police patrolling the roads that we were on a special mission, which enabled them to allow us to continue back to our own base.

Any other incidents of racial intolerance that you witnessed?

There were not many connected with the performance of our military duties. Once overseas, I think everyone concentrated on the prosecution of the war. To avoid incidents similar to on the train, when I left Jefferson Barracks as a young 18-year-old, I did everything possible to keep from using public transportation. I became aware of how much racial tension existed—how much segregation meant to people in certain parts of the country. Whether my parents brainwashed us or over-protected us in St. Louis is difficult to say. There was considerable subtle segregation in the city. I recall that we couldn't go to certain theaters. This wasn't earth-shaking since most people just went to neighborhood theaters because of the cost and distance. While concentrating on winning the war, I directed my efforts toward being respected as an American and sharing in the full citizenship that White Americans enjoyed. I tried to be the best I could. It took years for me to realize we Blacks had a long uphill battle. That brings me to a couple of incidents that occurred after the armed forces were integrated.

One story I remember was while I was at Keesler and had become an instructor pilot in the B-25. One of the pilots that had come there to school had been assigned to me for transition into the B-25. When he came in and we met, he excused himself and went to see the training officer and never returned. I understand he told operations that he wasn't going to fly with any "niggers." He insisted that they assign him another instructor pilot. The officer I admired—I think his name was Owens—was the operations officer, and as I have been led to believe, told our racist pilot he had been assigned to fly with a pilot and if he wanted to fly, he had to fly as assigned. This pilot still refused. A month and a half went by and they took his flight pay away; another month went by and his flight pay was taken away again. By the third month, his need for this back pay overpowered his disrespect for Black pilots. So he kind of tucked that tail of his between his legs and said, "Okay, I'll fly with any pilot I'm assigned to." He needed 12 hours of flying time, and I believe he flew them all with me. Another incident at Keesler that sticks in my mind happened in 1950. It involved the officers' swimming pool.

Integration had worked well under General Lawrence during my first year there, and as the result of his leadership, he had been moved to Lackland Air Force Base, Texas. In the minds of most Black officers and airmen there at Keesler, the new commander was not as forceful in applying the intent of President Truman's integration order. As a matter of fact, he set about to establish policies that were a setback from the previous year. This new policy was an attempt to re-segregate the officers' swimming pool, under the guise that he believed that Black military people would prefer to spend their leisure time together. To achieve that, he had converted one of the non-commissioned officers' (NCOs') pools for the use of Blacks.

He then issued an order that Black officers could no longer use the designed officers' pool. This order brought outrage from many officers—both Black and White—who set about to test the commanding general's (CG's) order. Our plan was that mixed groups with their wives or girlfriends would appear at the officers' pool in shifts, to test this admittance policy. I was one of three Black officers in the first group. I believe the other two were Theopolis Johnson, now of Los Angeles, and Fred Hutchins, of Atlanta. When we approached the entrance to the pool, a very large sergeant blocked our path to prevent entry. Very politely, he said, "Sir, Negro officers are to use the other pool," referring to the pool designated for use by all Black personnel, regardless of rank. My response was "Sergeant, move aside or I will have you court-martialed, and have your superior send someone here that outranks a captain to issue that order." He stepped aside and we went about our business.

Sometime later, three staff cars arrived, one containing the CG, from which a number of senior officers got out and stood looking, talking, and taking notes. At this point, I decided to be a show-off.

Not being much of swimmer, I climbed the ladder to the high diving board and began bouncing up and down. As I was looking around and saying to myself, "I'll show you," my foot slipped, and I found myself in mid-air heading for the water. Needless to say, going through my gyrations on the way down, I ended up parallel to the water and hit on my back. The pain was unbearable; however, despite this, we did manage to reintegrate one facility on base. There was never any mention of the incident again. I could go on, but after 42 years the system is working—not perfect, but working.

What was the toughest transition from WWII to flying in Korea?

I don't think there was any tough transition. You make adjustments each day to changing situations and conditions, to assignments and missions. In later 1948, 1 had gotten out of fighters, flying P-47s, and was flying B-25s at Keesler AFB. In 1950, 1 was assigned to a SAC unit at Fairfield-Suisun AFB, California [later Travis AFB], flying B-50s. I didn't like SAC and, of course, we were involved in Korea at that time. SAC crews were always flying off on extended missions and some may even have been to Korea. I figured if I had to go to Korea, I had to get back into fighters. I didn't have any interest in bomber tactics. I mean, something that sits up there and lets the enemy shoot at it was not for me. And, of course, by 1950, our jet fighters were faster and more maneuverable, which seemed more exciting and thrilling to fly.

Another thing, I never liked flying over water. I never had a great liking for any water I could not stand up in or drink from a glass, especially after my diving board escapade at Keesler. When I was flying in MAC and we would pass the Golden Gate Bridge and the Farallon Islands, going to Hawaii, I had problems dealing with all that water. I remember the first time I flew to Hawaii, that island looked so very small. It gets larger and larger each time I go out there.

What sort of special tricks did you guys use to do as the Tuskegee fliers?

I can't say it was special, but like most pilots we took great pride in our ability to fly aircraft. One of the more demanding aspects was formation flying. We would fly formations so tight that if the wind velocity was not too strong, a person could get out and walk from one end of one aircraft to another. We prided ourselves on how well we could tuck it in. I remember one time when practicing formation, I was on my buddy's wing so tight that he said, "Bill, your prop's going to hit my wing in a minute. Why don't you slide it back a little bit?" But I kept sticking it right up in there. So later, to get even, someone decided on the next flight that it was my turn to lead. We got up in the air and they began to pull in real tight.

You see, when you are in the lead aircraft, you can get the picture of what it is like and how critical the maneuvers are with the other aircraft pulled in real tight. I would try to speed up or turn or something like that, but they had their wings tucked up under my wings so tightly I couldn't escape. If I had tried, I could've touched the other planes' wings. Those formations required excellent reflexes, good hand-eye coordination, as well as teamwork.

They got even?

I would say they did, and they scared the hell out of me in the process.

Anything else like that you remember?

Well, yes, there are many others. One, in particular, occurred in Italy after the war ended. As I may have pointed out, the P-51 was the finest piston-engine aircraft ever built, and the easiest to fly, even upside down. Anyway, one of my comrades—who later went on to excel as an air force officer and commander—and I often flew in the same flight, would do low-level passes over other Allied airfields.

You could call into their control tower and request permission to buzz their field. In most cases, they would approve the request with the stipulation to "make it good." This particular day we were doing our little show over one of our B-17 bomb group bases, low, in a nice tucked-in formation. We thought we were looking good, but the control tower operator called on the radio and said, "You call that a buzz job? Our B-17s will do better than that." The remark kind of ticked us off, so we requested a re-run to show them. We came back across the field the next time, not more than 20 feet off the ground. John said, "Everyone tuck in real tight," and when I looked out at my wingman, he was upside down. Twenty feet off the ground! One mistake and you're dead. With the P-51, you could push forward on the stick when upside down and the aircraft would actually climb, and that is what he did to get enough clearance to roll back over. The tower operator screamed, "Oh, my God! He's going to crash." But Sam was good, and he was always testing the limits of the aircraft. As I said, he held his position in the formation across the field, pushed the stick forward, climbed a little bit up, maybe 20 feet, and rolled back over. The tower operator said, "That was a great buzz job."

What was life like when you got back after the war was over?

Many of us were sent back to Tuskegee after WWII. They really didn't know what to do with all the Black pilots they had produced.

Both the 332nd Fighter Group and the 477th Medium Bombardment Group had been deactivated in favor of a composite group made up of two squadrons from each group at Godman Field, Kentucky. This reduced the personnel requirements for fully qualified crews considerably. In keeping with the "separate but equal" status for Negroes, by sending the surplus back to Tuskegee, the War Department had created another monster. While some were lucky enough to get assignments as instructors, the remainder became assistant to the assistant to the assistant. In other words, multiple people were doing the same job. Though some outranked and were more qualified than their White counterparts, they were denied the opportunity under existing policy. With so many attempting to do the same job and trying to keep up their flying proficiency in the few aircraft allocated, we knew there was certainly considerable free time.

I remember how angry I became years later looking at some of my old slides and thinking that the War Department had sunk to a new low in human degradation when I would see a slide of George S. "Spanky" Roberts. Roberts was the first Black American selected for pilot training. He was the first squadron commander of the 99th Fighter Squadron; former deputy group commander and group commander of the 332nd Fighter Group. He had all of the needed credentials and demonstrated leadership for a key position, but suffered without a meaningful job. He was just one example of gross misuse of qualified military people. At any rate, the situation created new problems at Tuskegee Institute, where in their war preparation days, our military people were busy training and didn't have the time for social interaction. Now, it seemed they had more than necessary. We were now combat veterans, we had no studies to consume our time, we had no pressure on us; therefore one could devote his attention to personal pursuits, namely the girls in school.

This was very disruptive to the university academic atmosphere, and Dr. Patterson, who was responsible for bringing the pilot training program to Tuskegee, finally went to Washington, D.C., and used his influence and requested that the base be closed.

How long did you remain there after the call to close?

Once the Aviation Cadet Program was concluded, they began moving people to the new home of the Black air force at Lockbourne Army Air Field (later Lockbourne Air Force

Base) near Columbus, Ohio. I remained at Tuskegee until late August 1946, with a small contingent, to ferry out all of the aircraft and close the base. I was then transferred to Lockbourne AAF and reassigned to the 99th Fighter Squadron, again flying the P-47, until I left the service in January 1947, to attend St. Louis University.

This was just one of many breaks you had from the air force?

Yes. In September 1947, when I wanted to put in two weeks of active duty in the reserves, and since the Air Corps still operated under their "separate but equal" segregated military force concept, I was able to perform that duty at Lockbourne AAF with my old group. This time, however, I was attached to the 100th Fighter Squadron for training. There were a number of us shipped in from all over the country. It was like a homecoming, except that there were so many of us I was able to get only two flights in the P-47. It was while there for those two weeks that I found out that so many of us left the service that the group was now undermanned and that they would welcome anyone that wanted to come back in. I took the papers back to St. Louis with me and completed them so I could return to the service the end of next semester. Colonel Davis, later to become the first Black general in the United States Air Force and retired as a lieutenant general, told me on one of his trips to St. Louis that I should give him my application and that he would attach his letter of recommendation before it was sent to Washington.

I went on active duty in the spring of 1948 and was assigned to the 301st Fighter Squadron, again flying the P-47, until I was selected to be one of the early pilots to integrate the air force later that year. I was sent to Keesler Air Force Base, Mississippi, which was the same Keesler Amy Airfield discussed earlier, then under army control. One thing about Colonel Davis, and I am not sure it was by design, is that as we left Lockbourne, they made sure we were qualified in the type of aircraft at our new assignment whenever possible. That made our transition to the environment in an integrated air force much simpler.

You were not to stay in the air force for the remainder of your career?

No. After the swimming pool incident, conditions at Keesler became somewhat strained. I began to think that Black military people would never be given the opportunity or acceptance that President Harry S. Truman's integration order intended. In early 1950, I was one of many selected for non-flying status as part of a budget cutback. It was my opinion that the action was in retaliation to my defiance to General Mayo's swimming pool order of the previous year. I complained to the Department of the Air Force at the Pentagon, but to no avail. I believed that I was a good pilot and, by virtue of my instructor pilot ratings in two types of aircraft, I should have remained on flying status. I had no desire to stay in the air force in a non-flying position. I applied for release from active duty, to the University of California at Berkeley that fall, and headed west. When I arrived in Berkeley, I searched for a reserve assignment at Fairfield-Suisun Air Force Base—now Travis Air Force Base. While awaiting the start of the fall term, I secured an assignment in the SAC

Bomb Wing, flying the B-50 and the B-36. The units in those days had little or no use for the reservist, and getting flying time was hard if not part of the "in" group. My problem was even more difficult being a Black captain.

One day I was on base performing my active duty for training when I ran into Captain Paulus Taylor at lunch. He had been a personnel officer at Lockbourne. During our conversation, I had told him that I was dissatisfied with the problems I was having working my way into a B-50 crew. Some three or four days later, he called me at home and asked me if I would like an assignment in the MATS group he was personnel officer for. That assignment involved flying the C-47 (DC3), C-54 (DC4), and the C-97. I was qualified in the C-47, and because of their shortage of crews in the C-54 and my amount of flying time, I could expect to be checked out in that aircraft in the near future. This appealed to me since I had planned to test the commercial market in the future. The assignment was beautiful. Every time I was available, I could call in and get training days and was soon checked out in the C-47, and I then started my checkout in the C-54. It was great. I was flying all over the country and to Hawaii. In October, I received orders for recall to active duty. My wife and I had just had our first child, and the semester at UC would not end until mid-January, so I requested a deferment until then.

The operations officer for the 1704th was transferred to Japan just as I reported for duty, and I inherited his job. You can imagine the height of our nostalgia as many old friends came through on their way to the Far East. Colonel Davis, Captains Chris Newman, Hugh White; Lieutenants James Harvey, Edward Drummond, and Herven Exum were just a few of the Tuskegee Airmen to pass through.

I had my first experience in Korea and the Far East when I was sent over on temporary duty in the summer of 1951. We provided air evacuation for our wounded troops out of Korea and back to Japan, where they were evaluated for treatment and, where necessary, for evacuation back to the U.S. In 1952, I was assigned to flight service at Hamilton AFB, California, which did not require a family move at once. Our job there was to approve military flights out of any airfield not having their own clearing authority. While in assignment, I submitted my third request for helicopter training and, in the spring 1953, became the first Black helicopter pilot in the United States Air Force. This was a real experience and quite exciting, to fly a machine with no visible means of support. I became very intrigued with the capabilities of this up-and-coming means of air maneuverability and flew one on every opportunity I could get, till I left the air force again the end of the year.

So, at this point, you attempted to break into commercial aviation?

Yes, but this was not the first time. I had sent out resumes and many applications while in school at the University of California. However, with my new endorsement in helicopters, I believed my prospects of obtaining a position in the career I loved so intensely were much more promising. But the U.S. aviation industry was not yet ready to accept a Black flier. By this time in my life, I had acquired nearly 2,000 hours in fighters, bombers, various multi-engine transport aircraft, and helicopters, and yet my experience could not overcome racism.

One day, while walking in downtown San Francisco, I ran into Major Charles Bussey, who had been one of the Tuskegee Airmen who had remained in the army when the two services split. At the time, he was on the aviation staff at the Presidio of San Francisco. We had lunch together, and during our reminiscing, he pointed out that the army was high on helicopters and said that, if I wanted to continue flying them, I should transfer over to the army, since I had been unable to get a reserve assignment with the 4th Air Rescue Squadron at Hamilton AFB. The idea had merit, and after some investigation, I made the service switch in 1954. The one problem was the army would not accept me as a qualified pilot. In order to acquire my pilot's wings for them, I was required to attend helicopter flight school again at Fort Sill, Oklahoma. At the time, I had more helicopter time than my flight instructor. I truly believe that had I been White, they would have made the transfer based on my record and given me the necessary field training to become proficient in army field operations. After all, I was already qualified in the H-19 (Sikorsky S-55).

I remember my first flight in the army trainer. This young second lieutenant, whose name I chose to forget many years ago, took me out for that indoctrination ride and, after demonstrating the basic maneuvers, instructed me to take the controls and not to be afraid—he was right there with me. I handled the aircraft as smoothly as any pilot. This prompted him to ask if I had bootleg time. My response to him was I had none. Throughout the flight, as he demonstrated maneuvers and instructed me to perform them, he asked me the same question again. Each time I gave the same answer. I knew I was getting to him, but I was angry with the treatment I was getting after flying in two wars. He finally concluded the flight, and I believe made an unusual report in my flight folder.

The next day he decided to put me through some more advanced maneuvers by demonstrating auto-rotations. This is a maneuver where you cut the power and make an emergency landing into a small field. In this case, for safety reasons, they always used one of their emergency fields. After going back up, he requested that I attempt the same maneuver

RED TAIL PILOTS IN THE SUNSET

and not worry, because he was right there to help if I made a mistake. As I came around and chopped the power, I was really getting my jollies. We approached the ground, but I did not start to level the helicopter as he had done in his demonstration. Instead, I had decided to make the landing as we did in the air force. As he nervously reached for the controls, I shouted, "Get your hands off those controls!" I must have shocked the hell out of him, because he froze for a moment, and by the time he recovered, I was successfully on the ground. He sat there stunned for what seemed like eternity before he collected himself and repeated what had asked so many times. He said, "Mister, I am going to ask you for the last time, where did you get your bootleg time?" My response was the same as before: "I have no bootleg time."

In disgust, he directed me to take us back to the main field, where I parked and shut down the helicopter. He walked off without another word. As I returned to the ready room quite pleased with myself, I was approached by a sergeant, who directed me to report to the commandant. I walked in and smartly saluted as he told me to stand at ease. The commandant then proceeded to explain to me that the honor of pilot and officer in the army was based on truth and he was giving me one last chance to come clean and explain where I had acquired my bootleg time.

"Sir, I have no bootleg time."

"Well, where did you learn to fly like that?"

"In the air force, sir."

"So you do have some illegal time?"

My response: "No, sir, I do not." Oh, was I enjoying this! His next request was: "Mister, please explain yourself." "Sir, I was an air force pilot for over 11 years and flew H-19s in air rescue. I came into the army because of my interest in helicopters." He began to turn red. His next question inquired as to why I had not given him this information before. "Sir, you asked about bootleg time, and all of my time is duly logged in my form five, which I have been trying to convince the army was legiti for over three months."

If I was to continue in my vocation as a pilot, I had to play the army game. But after I arrived, I decided to show how stupid this racism game had been.

With shock, disbelief, or whatever was going through his mind, he directed me to bring my flight records to him as proof—which I did. The next day, when I reported to the flight line, I was again summoned and instructed to report to the school headquarters for further evaluation. I spent the next two days taking tests, and after the results were in, the school was instructed to graduate me with the next class. Since one class had just graduated, I then had to wait another four weeks. I had many confrontations before leaving the Army in 1957 with undertones of racism that could not be proven conclusively.

Was this when you began your next quest to break into commercial aviation?

Yes, but this time I had done my homework before leaving the service. I had already secured a position with Allied Helicopters, Tulsa, Oklahoma, spraying bananas in Central America and had believed this was going to be the beginning of a great future. That was not to be the case. The companies we were under contract to spray for, Standard Fruit and United Fruit, both of which had policies against socializing with the local people, and when I came along they forbade their people from socializing with me, so I was like a person that wasn't there, except when working.

How long did you stay there?

Not very long; just three weeks. I was just a replacement pilot. When I returned to Los Angeles for Christmas break, a friend and fellow Tuskegee Airman, Alvin Harrison, stopped by on his way back to Canada with his wife and my sister-in-law and talked me into helping him drive up. The trip turned out to be very advantageous to me and began another chapter in my flying career. While there, I was introduced to some of the pilots at Pacific Western Airlines during one of their holiday cocktail parties. It was after I returned to Allied Helicopters in Tulsa that I received a call at work from the chief pilot of Pacific Western, asking if I would like to come to work for them. I was due to depart for Central America within a couple of days and did not relish the idea of the conditions down there, so after considering the pay reduction for a few minutes, I accepted the offer and was off to a new life in Canada.

For the first time in my life, I was treated like a person and not some second-class citizen as I had been in the United States. The flying was exciting, the country was beautiful, and the people were what I sometimes considered overly friendly. With ideal working, social, and community conditions, I had found peace of mind and home.

When asked if I would return to active duty to serve in Vietnam, I said yes. I had been selected to attend the Command and Staff College at Fort Leavenworth, Kansas. After completing that school and taking a short Christmas break, I reported for duty at Fort Hood, Texas, as aviation safety and standards officer for the 268th Aviation Battalion in January 1967. The unit departed for Vietnam in the spring. I later moved to Saigon with the same job for the First Aviation Brigade.

After 13 months in Vietnam, I requested and received the same assignment in Germany. In Vietnam, the majority of my time involved investigating causes for our downed aircraft and aircraft accidents; in Europe, my major task was instrument training, check rides, and standards. I enjoyed teaching people the finer points in their flying technique. I demanded the best from them and took special pride in my own ability to demonstrate. I have heard that I have been referred to as the "Black Baron," because I demanded perfection. Whatever name the White pilots gave me, I felt that, after over 17,000 flying hours, of which 12,000 was in helicopters, I have made a major contribution to aviation and gained some respect for Blacks in the age of flight.

Freddie Hutchins, Tuskegee "Savior"

Chapter 3

The Black Messiah:
An Interview with
Freddie Hutchens

Freddie Hutchins was born in Blakely, Georgia, on September 16, 1920, back in the days, he explains, before everybody got a birth certificate. His family later moved to Donalsonville, Georgia. Hutchins graduated with honors from Douglas High School in Thomasville, Georgia. Freddie's father, Charles, had served in the American Expeditionary Force on active duty in World War I. At the insistence of his mother, Hutchins attended Tuskegee Institute. (Hutchins' mother died when he was a sophomore.) He completed his program in 1942. Despite having to work his way through college, he was active in campus activities, serving as the advertising manager for the *Campus Digest* and became a member of Omega Psi Phi. At Tuskegee, he studied agriculture and actually took a course from George Washington Carver, something for which he was very proud. His graduation year, the army commissioned the first five Black flying officers.

He went on to overseas duty with the Tuskegee Airmen where he experienced many incredible adventures, including the one he describes in the interview where, after being shot down, he is by a strange, unbelievable synchronicity, treated as a "Black Messiah."

When Freddie returned to the States in 1945, he went back to Tuskegee where he immediately became an instructor. He instructed there until they closed the field in 1946, after which he went up to Lackland AFB, and then to ROTC School in Texas for a training course. Finally, he would end up back at Tuskegee when the very first Air ROTC was established there.

Freddie became an early member of an organization known as Mach Busters Club, when he qualified for jets shortly after the Korean War. In his last active duty, Freddie was assigned as Executive Officer under Col. Marvin W. Glasgow II of the 444th Fighter

Squadron in Charleston, South Carolina. The squadron earned the distinguished award given by Hughes. After the war, he worked at General Electric and Lockheed.

This dear gentleman passed away in the summer of 1991, just before his 71st birthday. He is buried at Arlington National Cemetery and survived by two sons, Eric and Fred, Jr.

When did you see your first airplane?

It was when I was about nine or ten. I was born in southwest Georgia on a farm. I was always fascinated by airplanes. As time went on, we moved from living directly on a farm to a little farm town named Donalsonville. I built my first model airplane in that little town.

How did you do that?

Before I got to flying airplanes, I used to look for pieces of two-by-four and scrap wood. I'd whittle those down and make fuselages out of them. I'd use coat hangers for the struts and snuff cans to make my windshields. All went well until I tried to fly them, and I realized that they were a little bit too heavy to fly! I started off building a couple of different flying models and, after two or three failures, I built a Fokker D.VII aircraft.

Were you quite disappointed when you found a couple of those planes wouldn't fly?

Yes, I was.

How much did they weigh?

Oh, I don't know. I don't think I had one that weighed a pound. I was fooling around with rubber bands, and I finally learned that people put out special rubber bands to wind them up. I remember I built one that had a wingspan of about three feet. It was a one-blade prop with a counterbalance on the other end of it. I got that one to fly fifteen or twenty minutes.

What did you do to get it up in the wind?

Oh, that one had enough rubber in it. You could wind that doggone thing up a lot. The rubber band was about three or four times the wingspan and, if you wound it up real tight, that propeller would run a long time.

What did people think about your apparent obsession with flight?

A lot of people used to talk to my grand-daddy. They didn't want him to allow me to fool around with airplanes. They thought it was a waste of time, and that I was overly ambitious. The idea of fooling with an airplane was foolish!

What did your granddaddy say?

He was all supportive. When I was about twelve or thirteen, some man came to town with one of those barnstorming planes—it was a Stinson Reliant, a high-wing model that had four or five seats. He was charging people a dollar-and-one-half to ride. My granddaddy scrounged up two dollars and fifty cents. He didn't charge me full fare. That two- dollars-fifty cents, I think, was one of the best in-vestments granddaddy ever made.

Do you remember when you actually said, "I am going to be a flier?"

Yeah, yeah. I remember once somewhere around thirteen or fourteen, I was being re-sponsible for people gathering peanuts. That was one of the crops that grew on the farm almost every year. It was my job when the peanuts got ripe to take a mule with a certain type of plow, run underneath the peanuts, and sack them. Well, once, I got so carried away when what looked like every airplane in the whole Army Air Corps flew over, that I forgot about all my responsibilities. I just sat there and watched them. It took them about an hour-and- a-half to all fly over. I was still oohing and aahing when my granddaddy came on up. He got plenty irritated with me because he was paying the people out there by the day to pick up and gather peanuts, and I wasn't doing my job. He gave me a pretty good shellacking about that. I reminded him that I was going to fly one day. Later on, granddaddy came to see me get my wings. I went out to a local airport, rented a Piper, and took him up for a ride.

What was the toughest transition to Tuskegee?

I graduated from high school in 1938. I had applied at several colleges and was given a full scholarship to Johnson C. Smith, Marshall College, and Morehouse College in Atlanta. Then I was accepted at Tuskegee. Tuskegee had a reputation for students who came out with pretty good jobs, so I went there. I knew I was going to have to work my way through, and it was nip and tuck every quarter.

In 1939, they started the Civilian Pilot Training Program (CPTF). If you could get enough time in, you could end up with a private pilot's license. I couldn't qualify for that because I didn't have forty dollars. Still, every chance I would get I would talk to the people who were in the program. It wasn't long before Tuskegee was accepting people for military training.

Benjamin O. Davis, Jr. came to Tuskegee from Fort Benning. They didn't know what to do with him at Fort Benning. His daddy had given him a canary yellow Buick, and that wife of his would go round the base at Columbus with that top skinned back, and it just irritated the hell out of them there, so they figured out a place to farm him up to, and that was the ROTC at Tuskegee.

I was in the ROTC program, but I graduated before I could get my commission. I would have to go to school another two or three months— another quarter—and I didn't want to do that. I asked Davis if he would write a letter and request a waiver on three months' training because I already had a degree. He said, "Why don't you come and join the Army Air Force?" I said, "Look, I never applied, Lieutenant." He said, "You might just make it. I'd like to have you in my outfit." I applied, and eventually I was accepted and made it through.

Do you remember your last day of work?

I was working at the military base. They were building it in those days. It was built by a bunch of brothers, the McKissick Brothers. When I stopped working there, I was making $125 a week.

Did you almost think you couldn't afford to leave?

Yeah, that was a lot of change! But no, there wasn't much of that thinking, because I was bit by the bug. All of my life, ever since I can remember, I was fascinated by airplanes.

How did you feel when you were fighting the Germans? It must have given you a little extra adrenaline to think you were fighting this idea of a superior race.

Oh, it did. It did. We had very little knowledge of what Hitler's ideas were. Most Blacks at the time were not in tune with that type of news.

You were one of the first Tuskegee fliers to fly a P-51.

Yes. We had gotten word that we were going to get some airplanes. Finally, the operations officer walked by the tent one afternoon. He looked at me and said, "Hutchins, can you fly a P-51?" I said, "You bet your boots I can. Why? It's got a wing on it, doesn't it?" I was just mouthing off. I think the planes had arrived just a little quicker than the operations officer had expected. He said, "Okay, get your parachute on and grab nine more of your friends and meet me there at Base Operations in thirty minutes. Bring your own chutes."

"For what?" I said.

"You are going to pick up some airplanes."

"Is there a handbook on the airplane?"

"Yeah, there is one here."

"Where is it?"

"Oh, the Colonel has it."

We had to go down to one of the White

airbases where they were flying them—the 325th Fighter Group. They had the planes all lined up on the taxi-way. Someone placed numbers in a hat, so each one of us went into a hat and drew a number. One of the first lieutenants there climbed into the cockpit to give us a cockpit checkout. You know how confined it is around a cockpit. You can't get more than a few people close to it at once.

Finally, we got everything squared away. The lieutenant said, "Okay, are you ready to go?" I looked at the number that I had drawn. It was the first plane in the lineup. Nobody could get past me until I took that airplane up or moved it off the taxi strip. So that's how I got to fly the first flight.

What did you learn that day?

I learned a lot that day. I guess one thing that I learned was that the fuselage tank in the plane wasn't of original design. It was put in there after the plane was designed, to provide for extra fuel. Until you burned the fuel down into that fuselage tank, the airplane was kind of off kilter a little bit. I looked at the fuel gauge in the fuselage. It was way below the problem point. When I got out there, I proceeded to put on a show.

What did you do?

Oh, I buzzed the shit out of that air base, but one fellow thought I was going to hit him. He was driving an eighteen-wheel tractor trailer with eighteen P-51 engines on it. He saw me coming and panicked, so he jumped off the tractor trailer. The damn thing jackknifed, and what happened was he put eighteen airplane engines all over the ground.

Needless to say, we put on a show for the White boys. I initiated it, and we really beat this airfield up. When I got back over, I took a look down at the Old Man's tent. I was sitting there, and since I was at a reasonable altitude, I thought, "Shit, I may as well buzz him, too." I backed off and gave him a pretty good pass, and that tent leaned a little, and so I said, "Why don't I put it all the way down?" So I backed off. I got up to about ten-thousand-feet, about fifteen or twenty miles away. I got on a full head of steam and was coming down. As I did, it looked to me like I was looking up at the top of his tent. When I saw the Old Man,

I hit the war-emergency boost and, boy, did that plane jump. Then I could see it in my mirror. I pulled up and went down and then I started rolling right off the top of it.

When I came back, I did an awful lot of rolls. It turned out everybody had stopped working. The cooks had stopped cooking and everything had come to a standstill. When I finally came down and landed, all the mechanics and crew chiefs and everybody was all over the airplane. They were all asking me, "How did you like it, Lieutenant?" I said, "It's the greatest thing since girls." I pointed to it and said, "I'll name this one. This one belongs to me."

What did you call it?

"Little Freddie." See, when I left, I had this little wife who was pregnant. I said it was going to be a son, so I named the plane "Little Freddie."

You didn't get into too much trouble, did you? Or did you?

Yeah, when I was coming up from the white-line area, B.O. Davis's plane wasn't far from mine. I saw him standing there. Somebody had put his tent back up. He looked at me and said, "Hutchins."

I said, "Yessir." And he beckoned me over. He looked at me like I was a damn blithering idiot. He finally returned my salute and said, "At ease."

Then he said, "I bet that was you up there putting on that show." "Sir," I said, "you know this is one poker hand that I can't call." I used to play poker with the Old Man.

"It was you?"

"Yessir."

"Well, I think it's poor judgment." He was really mad. About that time his telephone rings and the commanding general was chewing his butt out, going and coming. He rapped him at attention from "Yes" to "No" to "Yes" and said, "Yessir, I wasn't involved. Yessir. No, sir."

I said, "Oh, shit." I was beginning to feel like my butt was going to get it now. When he finished talking, he said, "Do you know who that was?"

"No, sir."

"That was General Strother of the Fifteenth

Fighter of the 306th Fighter Wing. The general thinks that it was a pretty poor display of common sense, too."

"Yes. Well, I'm sorry sir."

Then he paused and said, "The General told me he wanted you all to be just as hot as you all want to be, but please you tell your people to get three or four hours in the damned airplane first (laughs)."

What about that tractor that jackknifed?

That was what started it. The commander of the outfit had called the command and told them what the hell was going on. The driver of the truck thought he was going to get killed and, hell, I wasn't going to hit him.

Was it a White guy driving the truck?

Oh, yeah, this was a White outfit.

You started out to say a little while ago that you showed those White people you could do it. Obviously, you felt a need to prove yourself, because people didn't believe you could do it.

Yeah, one of the things that stood up above them was that we had a whole lot more flying time than the White fliers did. See, they would come in and have anywhere between four and ten hours in the operational-type airplane. They'd sent the White pilots overseas as re-placement pilots. But, at the time when we were sent overseas, I've got to say that I was an original—we had up to 200 hours in combat-type aircraft.

The prizefighter Joe Louis had a farm up in Michigan not so far from the airfield, and since we flew seven days a week, we could go up there and bug the people who were up there riding horses—watch them fall off their horses. Also, we would fly underneath the bridge that connected Michigan and Canada—the Fort Huron Bridge. I think I hold the record for that. I took six airplanes under there at one time.

Six airplanes under the Port Huron?

Yes, at center span. We had a formation of six. That was foolish on my part because we didn't have that much room. I backed them up—way back up— and I told the pilots they ought to pack it in real tight. They did pack it in real tight! I don't think we had room to breathe. I figured we had enough clearance to get through there, and we did. Word got around, and when it did, word came back that we would do no more things like that again.

Was Freddie Hutchins a little bit of a hell-raiser when he was younger?

A lot of people called me kind of loose-goosey, but I wasn't. I was really a very intense person, but one who didn't show it. I would develop some wisecracks to sort of take some of the apparent intensity off things.

What do you think you didn't want to show?

Well, I don't know. I would just guess, I suppose, that it was because this experience was all new to us. We were the first of our kind—we didn't see any others before us—so we had no rules for comparison. At that point, all my instructors were White; the instructors at Tuskegee were White, too.

Did you have any trouble with White instructors?

I didn't. I didn't feel any indication of trouble. Most of the instructors were southerners. But we had a few good laughs sometimes.

Like what?

Oh, I had one instructor in Basic. His name was Gabriel C. Hawkins. Of course, Gabe was a very good instructor. But one day we went out there to AT-6s, and he did something that was cardinally wrong. He didn't open the fuel tanks and stick his fingers down into the tank—the wing tanks. If you couldn't feel fuel in there, you'd take the tops off, and put fuel in there until you felt fuel. Anyway, he didn't have much fuel in there, and he took off. As soon as he did, he got to about a hundred or two hundred feet in the air, and the damn thing quit on him.

He tried to turn it back into the main airfield, which was wrong. The book says, "Go straight ahead." Anyway, he lived, but he got his face cut up so badly it wasn't even funny. It so happened they needed some special kind of blood for him, and there was one man on that base with that special kind of blood. That someone looked Senegalese. Do you know what a Senegalese looks like? They all start around six-foot-six. And they've got no fat on them—call it "muscle."

Well, this chap had the kind of blood that

Hawkins needed, but Hawkins said, "Ah, hell, just let me die." His wife said, "Don't put that damn blood in him." The hospital commander was also a Southerner, but a very humane person. Well, he rode the fellow from Senegal over there, and they knocked out Hawkins, then rolled this Black person up beside him and said, "Put in a little fuel."

Hawkins was then sewed up by a young black doctor who had graduated from Howard. The goose he gave Hawkins was so small that today you couldn't tell whether it was a scar or a little burn. And this man went and put 250 stitches in him.

Anyway, Hawkins lived. But he didn't want any children after that. He didn't want any Black babies.

Did he tell you that?

Yeah, he will tell you that now.

Is he still alive?

I don't know if he is now. Well, I know he finished off his tour up at Memphis State. I have been to Memphis State several times to see him. Every time I come up there, I give him a call, and he comes out to the airport to visit with me. He made full colonel.

In 1951, I was over in Korea, but I came back to Japan. I needed some uniforms, so I went to the military base to buy me some uniforms. This damn burly sergeant up there says, "You can't take any uniforms."

I said, "Sir, to you, damnit! Why can't I buy any uniforms?"

"Because Major Hawkins said you couldn't buy any uniforms."

"Where does it say that?" Hawkins had put out a memo that no uniforms were to be sold to people over in Korea because there was a shortage. I thought that was one hell of a note.

"Is this Major Hawkins anywhere around here?"

"Yeah, why?"

"Get him on the phone. I want to talk to him."

I knew who it was. I read the sign that said "Gabriel C. Hawkins." I didn't think they'd have but one Gabriel C. Hawkins in the whole air force. He was at lunch when I called him up and told him I wanted to buy some uniforms, that they wouldn't sell me any. Then I told him who I was.

"What in the hell are you doing over here?"

"I'm over in Korea."

"Wait, don't move a thing. I will be right down there." He stopped what he was doing and came right down to the office. He told the sergeant, "Let him buy some uniforms." The sergeant looked straight at him and said, "Are you going to violate your own directive?" Hawkins said, "To hell with it."

After we got the uniforms, we went to his house. He was living on the base, and his wife fixed up a place for me. We got to talking and laughing about the blood episode. It turned out that Gabriel and his wife had had three kids. The kids were falling apart when they learned about their parents' stupidity. At the time Gabe and his wife were damned serious— they weren't going to have children, but as it turned out, they went to a party, I guess, and forgot about that damn rhythm method—and she got herself pregnant.

As a consequence, they ended up with some kids. All of them were blond-headed and blue-eyed, just like the parents. We laughed and laughed about that. He laughed, too. He said he just didn't know.

We all laugh about it. Every time I'd see Gabe he would laugh about it, because he had made three big mistakes that day: One, he did something he'd told us not to do: Don't ever take off until you check the fuel in your tank and you can feel it in there, and two, if the engine quits shortly on take-off, don't try to come back to the field. Try to go straight ahead, and the third one, he didn't want any of that "doggone nigger blood" in him. But he had no qualms about telling anybody the whole episode. He was saying, "You can understand. Hell, we didn't know any different. We were doing what we were taught."

What was the most surprise you saw from somebody who saw you Black fliers flying?

In 1945, I think, they had some P-51s down at Moody Air Force Base, and they wanted to take them to a base in New Mexico. We took off and went down to Valdosta, Georgia. We had special buses pick us up. I think there were twenty-five of us back there, and our job was to fly the airplanes. They had looked to Tuskegee because we were P-51 pilots, so it was logical we transport planes down there.

But the base commander found out who we were, and he was just wringing his hands. When they finally had found out that all of us were people of ethnic descent—or whatever you call it—they said, "Don't you let them go down and pick them airplanes up."

It turned out they couldn't stop us from picking them up. Finally, the guy said, "They're out there on the highway." The commander said, "Call the state patrol. They can stop them." The guy said, "No, I wouldn't do that."

They decided to let us go, but they alerted the people at Moody that there were twenty-five of us coming down to pick up those airplanes for flight. So Moody was waiting for us. We got there a little after dark. We wanted to get up early the next morning and get a good start.

The trip had three legs to it. For the first leg we were going to stop in Shreveport, Louisiana. We had a little trouble getting the airplanes—just smilin' nit-pickin' stuff. The planes hadn't been flown in a good length of time, so it was maintenance stuff here and there. They finally got us off the ground, and we got into tight formation.

We went by the Tuskegee Army Airfield, and asked permission to pass in review. They said, "You're cleared to pass once from the northeast to the southwest." We came down that runway right down in front of the buildings that were packed there like sardines. We could fly some formations! We put on a good show and came back in line and buzzed a couple of times. Then I took off, pulled out of formation and did my little slow roll off the deck. I had done maybe a six-point hexagon. You would go until you got maybe six different angles within the 360-degree angles.

At last, when we pilots came out of formation, everybody was out in the streets. We had gone back up into formation and passed up over there in formation. We waved our wings and went out past the annex and went on into Louisiana. We did what those boys do in NASA, when they taxi in formation: When one canopy comes up, all of them come up. Well, we had been used to doing this, so I taxied up in front. This fellow, who was sitting up there giving me these signals on how to park the damn thing, watched. The airplanes came down, landing one right after the other—

you could hardly tell where one wing ended and another began. We were that close to-gether. I just reached up there and shut the airplane down. The man that was parking me jumped up on the wing. As he jumped up, I unbuttoned my oxygen mask. I could have sworn he had seen a ghost. He fainted and fell right on that damn wing!

By that time, we were all getting out of the planes. Everybody looked to see us. They had troopers out there, and the base commander met us. He said, "We don't know if you are going to stay here tonight." I said, "We can't continue on. It will be dark by the time we get to the next station we planned to go to." We were going to Fort Worth the next day and we were going to stop there. Finally, they put us—not in the officer's quarters, but down on the other end of the field where they had all the other Black troops. They had a nice little hut, and the beds were clean.

They couldn't feed us in the Officer's Club, so they brought us a truck and sent us down-town. They were clearly not as hospitable as they were in Valdosta.) They sent us down-town to a nice little restaurant some Black person had. We had some beautiful steaks and, of course, the base picked up the tab.

A couple of the fellows decided to look around downtown Shreveport. They didn't do a thing wrong, but a cop picked them up down there and put them in jail. "Niggers impersonating an officer." The cops called us out at the base, and the base commander said, "Yes, we got some here." He asked for their names, and the guy gave him the names. He said, "I'll send someone down to pick them up."

The base commander called me down at the bivouac area, where we were bunking and said, "I think they've got a couple of your troops down there. The local police picked them up for impersonating an officer."

I had to chuckle about it, because I had told the sons-of-bitches to stay put, so the provost marshal went down and picked them up and brought them back. One of the fellows was explaining. I said, "You don't have no explanation for this. I told you from the damn beginning that we are here to ferry airplanes, not to socialize."

The next morning, we got up and were getting ready to meet. The base commander came out and said, "You can't take off in this kind of weather."

"What do you mean, General?"

"This weather is below minimum. This is below the instrument flight rules."

"Yeah, I understand that," I said, "but we are leaving here."

"Well, I will have to write you up."

"Fine, but I've got my rebuttal."

We had to leave because they couldn't give us the accommodations suitable to commissioned officers in the air force. That's why we decided to go to the next state.

We went and lined up and got on the airplanes and went over to Fort Worth. I don't know if you know, but in Texas and Oklahoma and Kansas, they've got no trees, no rock, no nothing to stop the Arctic wind. When it's bad, they call it a "Great Northern." Well, while we were there in Fort Worth, we had one, so we were stuck there. The people were nice, though.

You never got in any trouble for taking off against orders.

Oh, no.

What was the most important thing you learned in the military?

Respect your own abilities and make sure you know your own limitations and, above all, be honest with yourself. We have had people who got into trouble because of just that one thing. You know, when I was telling you about how I had buzzed the base command and the tent fell down? What I didn't tell you was that I had gone upstairs, and I was ready to run that airplane out. I knew what it would do. I didn't do it on the deck the first time. I had plenty of altitude, if there was a mistake.

I didn't feel I was in any jeopardy. Every time I'd pull a roll on the deck, I would always —before I'd start my roll—pull the nose of the airplane up. So, when I started my roll, the nose of the airplane was going up by two degrees—or about fifteen or twenty degrees, maybe. That gives you some margin of error, if you have to fall out.

What was your favorite air tactic? Was it the hexagon?

No, one of the things I used to like to teach when I came back after combat was the cube-

and-eight. With cube-and-eights, you start off and take an intersection. When you get up and start looking at the ground from up there, you can almost see yourself pulling off squares. What you want to do with a cube-and-eight is pull up and go just like you are going to go into a loop. And you go through the loop and, as you come through, while you are inverted, you roll on your way down and go into a second loop, coming back up. Then, when you roll it out again, that's a cube-and-eight. That means you become inverted in the airplane.

Let's talk about going to war.

We left Selfridge Air Force Base. That was, I think, Christmas Eve in 1944. We came out on a special troop train and went to Newport News, Virginia. That was where we bivouacked until we could get overseas.

How did you feel that night?

For a time, we felt a lot of mystery to it. I remember that first night we got to the Patrick Henry Hotel. Some of the people came up to B. O. Davis and wanted him to come out and shake hands and he wanted to bring some of his boys. But they said, "What are they doing?" "They want to sit anywhere. They want to sit in the movie theater."

"They aren't sitting where they are supposed to be sitting."

Davis looked straight up and said, "I guess you'll just have to leave them alone, because my troops are going overseas, and we have received our arms. I don't think it would be wise for anybody to get into any argument here while they are sitting in the theater."

Later on, in January, we finally got overseas. I think we had two ships per squadron. We would have these submarine drills, and they would come out and blow the whistle. We would, of course, come running on deck and put on our Mae West life jackets and crash helmets on, go through the walkway and get into lifeboats.

We found out that the boat we were on had a thousand pounds of mercury fulminate fuses on board. Those fuses have got a problem with flash point. That's where you only need a little friction before the things will explode. But, once we knew what we were riding on, we realized there was no point in trying to get off that thing in an emergency because, if we got hit by torpedoes, shit, we would never know what hit us.

What was the worst practical joke you witnessed?

It wasn't really a practical joke, nor was it on me. But I remember this time we were outside of Nome, Alaska. This was after the integration of the air force. We had about three-and-a-half to four hours of nighttime per day. Of course, we dug out slit trenches. We would go out and use them for discharge of body wastes. One fellow had to go early in the morning. The wind was blowing something awful, and the temperatures were about minus sixty degrees. I don't know what the chill factor was, but it was cold. We were in layers of clothing. So this fellow started breaking down his one pair of pants over one pair of pants. When the wind told him he was down to his bare bottom, he squatted over that slit trench and, all of a sudden, you could hear him cussing. He didn't get the last pair of pants down. He had to live in that damn stuff. It wasn't funny to him, but it was funny to us.

In Alaska, the sun was bright as hell off the melted snow and ice and could create problems. Once when we had completed bivouac, which was seven to ten days, we would have to do our survival work. After that, we all came back and we were all sunburned. Of course, the Whites experienced all that reflection and glare out there as well, and they burned, too. But my skin was actually peeling. Just like a damn snake getting a new hide. Anyway, the first time somebody noticed it, he said, "Hey, look here at Freddie. He's been burned, too." He was dead serious. He didn't think Negroes could get sunburn.

What was your first sortie like? Were you apprehensive?

I wasn't so apprehensive. I figured it had been a long time since I had been in an airplane. We got a few hours as refresher. I don't know what the first mission was about. But we were later patrolling up by Naples Harbor. Then we moved farther up and were flying out of Naples.

What was the first dogfight you got into?

We were flying long-range escort for B-47s. We spotted a few planes. I was flying B.O. Davis's wing at the time. We spotted these planes up there at about nine o'clock high. They were coming around us. "Bandits at eleven o'clock high." Pretty soon we said, "Bandits at twelve o'clock high." They first started off calling them bogeys until they were identified. They were in formation just like we were, and they were trying to catch us from the top. They'd always be over our head. We never could get above them. That day we were really ready to go. B.O. Davis hollered, "You with me, men?" Everybody said, "We got you covered. Go ahead and lead."

"How about you Freddie?"

"Colonel, I am right on your wing."

"Let's go get them."

"Charge, men." And we did.

We were dispatched from Italy down to Athens, Greece, and we didn't know what was going on down there in the first place. Later, it became known to us what the purpose was. The British were going to parachute into Greece and then drive the Germans back north. They were using us to go down there and soften up the anti-aircraft. We went down there several times. Every time we went down there, we lost airplanes. I don't think I was on the last flight that went down, but I got hit with ground fire. They were shooting up, and it just exploded at about the same time I was there. I got hit with 20mm ground fire. The airplane was struck everywhere it could possibly be hit.

I realized that I wasn't going to make it home. I started making tracks as far away as I could from that airport. The wingman saw me and he followed me. I nursed that airplane until it just wouldn't go anymore. About then, I slammed into a mountain near Athens, just north of the city. The wingman saw the Germans making tracks over there to where I was. The wingman thought I was dead, but he gave me the benefit of the doubt.

Then some sympathizers got there. They just put me on one donkey and loaded up another donkey with my parachute and other paraphernalia. They started making tracks up into the hills. It was known the Germans weren't going to come back up to the hills. But that wingman kept the Germans off me.

Who was your wingman?

A young man named Roger Romine. He got killed later on. But he stayed there until he couldn't stay any longer.

He just shot at them?

Yes, every damn time those Germans would start out, and it looked like they were headed my way, he just turned those six fifty-caliber guns in their direction and that kept me from being captured.

What do you remember about that trip up the mountain?

After about an hour of it, I started hurting like hell. I took a look at my mouth in a mirror and my teeth were raggedy. I was spitting up blood. I had also been hit in one of my legs. It was a nick in one of the bones, and I broke my jawbone and my ankle. I just took my fingers and put my teeth back in place. You see, when I had hit the ground, I hit the gun sight of the airplane. At the time, I was doing about 256 miles per hour. That's a pretty sudden stop! Well, I guess you don't stop suddenly, you bounce, so the airplane bounced and made me accelerate through the air. When that happened, the plane broke into pieces and the cockpit rolled over about three times and it stood upright.

What did you think?

I realized that Saint Peter wasn't there with his harps and everything to anoint me and let me come on in. I looked around and thought, "Well, hell, it wasn't quite my time."

I reached in back of the canopy—what was left of it—and pushed it open and got out. I ran about twenty-five yards and fell flat on my damn face. Then the underground resistance people picked me up. They realized that this man, Romine, was keeping the damn Germans off of them, so they came in.

When I realized that I was safe with them— that they were friends and weren't going to kill me—I felt a lot better. They moved me near a little village and hid me in a haystack until it got dark. I looked up at my watch: it was about nine o'clock when they got me out of the haystack and put me in a little canoe with two men in it. Those sons-of-guns rowed from nine o'clock in the evening until three or four the next morning. We made land somewhere but, by now, I was really beginning to hurt.

Then we came into a little village and the whole village was out there. They were just about as ecstatic as can be. They all wanted to see me. The Germans had apparently come up to this little village just a couple of days ago. They had taken all the food that these people had. But then, that night I arrived, they had about a three-hundred-pound swordfish come taxiing in up there in the lake, grounding, and couldn't get back out there into deep water. They didn't have any food and then, all of a sudden, by coincidence they did. I didn't have a damn thing to do with it. This damn three-hundred-pound swordfish just came in. He was thrown up against the sand and couldn't get back out with the tide. Now there was plenty of swordfish for everybody there in the village. From other villages, people brought in staples like some cornmeal, beans—and we ate. We stayed at that place for one day.

A lot of people were up there, and they spoke that I was the Messiah. It was the luck, of course, but they thought that the case because this being came there about the same time the fish came, so there was a connection.

The next morning, about first light, a kid walked up to me. He spoke perfect English. He was born and reared in Detroit. He and his family had come back up for a vacation and had gotten caught over there during the war. You could tell he was an American. He had American written all over him. He was a redhead from Baltimore, Maryland, and he had green eyes. He was about six-foot-three and weighed about two hundred and a half. When he walked up to, and all he said was, "All I need is your name, rank, and serial number." I gave it to him. He said he was going to send word back that I was safe.

Lee Archer II, Tuskegee pilot

Chapter 4

The Sky's No Limit:
An Interview with
Lee Archer II

Lee Archer exudes confidence, not the youthful kind he describes in the interview he had, but a confidence born of skill and remarkable achievement.

Born in Yonkers, New York, in 1919, he received degrees from UCLA and New York University and, in addition, he worked on a doctorate degree.

Despite the travails of racial segregation and prejudice, described in the interview, he prevailed, and graduated in 1943 from Tuskegee's Army Air Force units, and became a member of the 302 Fighter Squadron, under the 332 Fighter Group.

Considered by most the first Black "Ace," he shot down five airplanes. He also destroyed six on the ground. One of several "To Triple," which meant he destroyed three Me-109s.

He retired as a lieutenant colonel in 1970. In 2007, President George W. Bush awarded him the Congressional Medal of Honor. He also holds the Legion of Honor Chevalier.

The heights of his achievement in air were equaled, perhaps, by his stunning achievement outside the service. He was involved with a group that bought Beatrice International Foods. He also served as Corporate Vice President of General Foods.

Tell me, how did you get interested in flying?

From childhood, I was one of those kids who made model airplanes that resembled those Flying Aces from World War I, and I just plain liked airplanes.

My family had a summer place up by Saratoga, New York, located by this private airfield and these small little private planes use to fly in there all the time. I just liked to watch them land and take off.

Did anybody show you any kind of special kindness up there at the private airfield and let you do anything?

No, no, far from that. There was this feller there that was flying people around the field and he tried to run me off, but my father had a terrible temper and told him a thing or two. He responded by giving me a ride (laughs)

Describe your father's appearance. Was he a big guy?

No, no, he was maybe five-foot-ten or five-foot-eleven and weighed maybe 190 pounds or so. He was an active businessman and had six or eight independents working with him.

Were you surprised when he acted that way? How did you respond to that?

I told him I couldn't get a ride, (laughs) He was up there for the races, and that's why we had a plane up there.

He raced for fun, number one, and during summer kids get out of school and they used to just hang around New York City doing nothing all summer, so he had a place up there near Saratoga on Copper Street, and we'd go up there. There were taxi drivers up my father knew, and he used to gamble up there. In fact, he gambled quite a bit.

Sounds like he was a colorful character.

He was, and he raised me alone. My mother died when I was young, and I didn't have her around those early days and I was the only one around in the family then and most of the other kids around there were on their own, too.

What was the biggest lesson from him? Did he crack down on you? What did you learn from him growing up?

Well, he cracked down on me all the time. He owned a bar in New York at one time. I was a teenager at the time, and I couldn't get a drink anywhere in New York City, and there was no way I could get away with it from him. I couldn't hang out on the corner, and he would worry the cops would get me so he was sensitive to that. He was a politician, and I remember he was on the state Board of Elections and he had a democratic vote. He had other sidelines, which were his avocations, I guess.

What did he think about your flying once you got into it to any extent?

My father flat-out didn't like the idea of me going into the service at all. I volunteered and they refused me. You have to realize he had fought in WWI. He served in WWI, and he served in his unit and then he came back to the States, and was part of a Black organization of federal employees in WWI, but he refused to become a corporate guy.

Which battalion?

It was Fourth Battalion. This was after the Spanish-American War.

Did your dad like to recall that experience?

No, he only mentioned it one or two times in his life and said that was enough for us. His military experience made me think I could be first in any flying military. It was something I wanted to do, the idea of flying, not just flying model airplanes.

Do you remember the favorite plane that you built?

It was any airplane, but usually WWI airplanes. I liked airplanes of that period. None of the fliers I knew had that hobby. I just spoke to somebody today who remembered how much I used to like airplanes.

Let's talk about your training. Where did you go?

You know the system, I applied for Army Air Corps, and I took the test and came out really, really well on the test. I went down with these White friends of mine, and they balked at my papers of mine. I did better than the fellas I went down there with, but a couple months later they got called up for the Army Air Corps, but I didn't, so I went down to see what happened. I figured there must have been a mistake as I knew they needed fliers. They informed me that they hadn't sent my test through, because between 1925-1930, in the military, they had found out that colored men did not have the ingredients: capability, intelligence, leadership, coordination or ability to handle an airplane. Yak, yak, yak, they went on. I asked for the study and no, no, they couldn't get that study. We have that study now and this study actually stated there that colored men, African-Americans are inherently inferior. It claimed they also believed they knew that they were, and that they didn't have the necessary qualifications. They didn't have the strength; they didn't have the bravery, and it goes on and on. This is after African-American men had served in every war since the Revolutionary War, and they couldn't even be honest. This just infuriated me.

I told them then I didn't give darn what the study said, and I wanted to keep my papers, so I left there and suddenly I got a call from the draft. I informed the draft that I was leaning toward joining because of what my father said: "Hell comes from emergency."

I was in political science class, and I knew what that what would happen to these people in the war would be terrible, and I really wanted to fight and serve the country.

What year was this?

This was 1941.

And you knew, you really knew, what was going on with the Germans and the concentration camps?

I didn't think, and my belief was that Hitler was watching the Jews, and not colored people. But anyhow I contested the call up and they said "No, you volunteered for the service." "No," I said, "I volunteered for the Army Air Corps" and they said, "The Air Corps and Air Force is not accepting now." And they shipped me off to a place called Camp Wheeler, Georgia, for the 16th Battalion. That was located in Macon, Georgia. So I was in the 16th Battalion, where I became a telegrapher. I was very good at it. Meanwhile, I was making up my mind what to do. Incidentally, the 16th battalion at Camp Wheeler was segregated. and they had a thousand people on it, and they had us [African Americans] off to one side about a mile from the rest of the people on the base. They went back, got all the people who had applied. They called it, "Give our boys a chance." They went back to all those people, and said, "Hey, do you still want to fly missions?" Of course, we said "yes."

They thought they would have done better if they found a bunch of drunks on a street corner, but they said to these African American boys, "Hey, you want to be pilots, you'll be starting from scratch." They built a separate little station, whereas normal cadets, some were shipped to another base. With us, we all stayed in one place. The mistake they made was that they manned this training command with a bunch of southern officers. The commander of the base was so bad.

What was the worst thing that happened to you personally there in terms of insults and mistreatment?

Nothing. I ended up being a Cadet, the first captain in my class. They assumed that these officers, if given a terrible time, would wash out. Some of them did. I remember that Harris told me once that the idea is to get rid of some of us. "But I'm going to train you the Army Air Corps procedure to fly. I'm going to see that you can fly, I'm going to pass you, then it's the government's problem," A lot of us got through that way.

Did any of these guys ever do anything that was inspirational?

Well, the guys that inspired me were the black pilots who taught us in Primary. In Primary we had Black pilots. These were the first Black men to have licenses to fly and to become instructors in America. Some of them couldn't even learn here—they had to go over to France to learn to fly. There were people like that who had learned to fly and built their own airplane and then flew across the country.

Give me something about Chief Anderson.

Yes, he flew Mrs. Eleanor Roosevelt, and she said to her husband she didn't see why young Black men in America couldn't fly in the Army Air Corps. That put together with the election made a difference.

Tell me a Roscoe Draper story.

A very simple story about him was that he was my instructor in Primary. He took me out, maybe two-and-one-half hours to fly, on the third ride, I think it was. He gave me hell from the time we took off, for everything I did. And I was thinking the worst.

Then he told me to take the airplane back to the hanger. He told me I was a danger to society. He climbed out of the plane, stood firmly on the ground, and told me, "Okay, you take it up this time." Then I knew I had passed the flying test.

So what do you think his strategy was, was he teasing you, was he just a tough guy?

He had decided that I could solo the airplane and could fly it as much as he needed to see to know I was able. But he told me not to think I was a hot shot because, at the time, I thought I was pretty hot. But he beat me down, so I didn't feel like such a hot shot anymore. Then he told me, "Okay, big shot, you can secure the airplane by yourself." He was one of my favorite people in the world, to date, as far as I'm concerned.

You did something like 187 missions, didn't you?

No, I did 169. People have been adding to that.

Tell me the time you were most frightened.

This is a problem—something I hate. Maybe there's something wrong with me. But they'd tell me the dangers and I'd think why the hell are they telling me in the first place? But then I'd look around the table at the four guys. Maybe, one was a little shy, but it was never me. Maybe it was because I was nervous and didn't realize it, but I'd be coming out to the airbase to go on a mission. it just never struck me that way.

Did you ever have any rivalry with your fellow pilots, any bets or competitions?

No, only the pilots that I considered my best competitors. I'd be lying if I didn't. And the other fellow was a fellow by the name of Wendle Koontz. He and I would fly together, and the others would kid us, of course, because we would fly a mission every day, if we could. Guys would bring airplanes back and we would go and get the airplane and fly.

How many kills did you have, total?

Five. Six on the ground but killed in the air, five.

Can you describe one of the kills for me?

It was just the same thing, we were coming back from an escort mission, and saw an airplane that was taking off from an airfield near a lake. We just happened to meet up with a bunch of Me-109s coming over, and I latched on to one of them. He kept trying to get away, kept on going, and finally I got a hit. He popped out of the airplane, and the plane started rolling. I just kind of circled him till he hit the ground. I didn't want anybody else to shoot him down. I didn't want anyone else to get the idea the guy hanging in the parachute was a target. We had heard about that. Someday, I thought, you may be hanging from a parachute. The thing about it was he gave me no choice. You see these movies where the guy's coming back. I came back, and all I could think of then was that he was doing the same thing for his country I was doing for mine.

What would you like most to be remembered for?

Well, it had nothing to do with the service, except that I consider the fact that the 332nd during WWII was responsible for integration of the service, which was the first integration in America, even before the Civil Rights movement, before Jackie Robinson, and things like that. In fact, right now we're celebrating the 50th anniversary of that, which took place under Harry Truman and Executive order

9981, in 1948, which banned segregation in the military.

So that's one of the ones you are most proud of, right?

I'm most proud of that. I'm proud of having been a command pilot. There are lot of things. But I'm also very happy that I've had opportunities since then.

Acknowledgments

Special thanks to Gene and Janice Coburn, Joanie Eppinga, and Julie Klein.

www.ingramcontent.com/pod-product-compliance
Lightning Source LLC
Chambersburg PA
CBHW051840090426
42736CB00011B/1904